BILL LEGGATE'S STORY

The life of William Bennie Leggate 1922 –

This is a memoir of my life and times, but it's not only about me and my life; it's about my hometown of Strathaven, some of the people who lived around the town and some of its characters and stories.

"Not to know what happened before you were born is always to remain a child. For what is a man's life if it is not linked with the life of future generations by memories of the past." - Marcus Tullius (Cicero).

© Copyright 2014 by William Leggate.
Copyright Holder John Leggate.
All rights reserved.
Printed and bound by CPI Group (UK) Ltd, Croydon, CR0 4YY
Published in hardback 2014 by www.leggatefamily.com
Project manager and writing consultant: Neil Jefferies
Contact: piracy1999@aol.com
Edited by Elizabeth Hojlund
Contact: info@elizabethhojlund.com

ISBN: 978-0-9931135-0-5

The front cover photo was taken at Paradise Beach, Nassau

More photos can be seen at www.leggatefamily.com

This book is dedicated to
Marjorie "Madge" Constance Leggate 1922 – 2013.

"Her time had come and she will now join the pantheon of immortal and extraordinary women whose influence is felt for many years after their passing. Throughout her long life our mother brought compassion and warmth to the lives of untold numbers of people and her legacy will undoubtedly influence the direction of generations yet to be born."

John Leggate 27 July 2013

Notes

Strathaven (Old) station was the terminus of the Hamilton & Strathaven Railway which was later taken over by the Caledonian Railway. The station was replaced by Strathaven North which then became a terminal of the Hamilton & Strathaven Branch of the Caledonian Railway. It opened in 1904, closed temporarily during World War One, and closed permanently at the end of World War Two. Strathaven Central station, on the Darvel & Strathaven Railway, closed in 1964. Nowadays Strathaven is a bustling country town. Many people travel from nearby and faraway places to visit its beautifully maintained public parks with its splendid miniature railway and key events such as the Gala Day and the Hot Air Balloon Festival. As you wander through the streets of Strathaven it feels good. It's very picturesque, with little humpy bridges spanning tiny watercourses that babble their way through the town. The town's "jewel" is its shops, and what you get in Strathaven's shops is a tradition that goes back to the 19th century. For instance, Alexander Taylor, the bakers, has been run by the same family since 1820. Strathaven may be a small place but small is very, very beautiful.

Thanks to The Good Soup Guide for their guidance

Lanarkshire is the busiest manufacturing and most populous county of Scotland, and it is situated round the river Clyde; hence its name Clydesdale. It contains Glasgow, Hamilton and Airdrie, all owing their importance to the rich coal and iron fields of the county. The population is about one million two hundred thousand.

"Jack's Reference Book, 1919"

Albany is the capital of New York State. It is on the Hudson River and is the second oldest city in the USA. Initially, Albany was just a couple of Dutch trading posts, one called Fort Nassau in 1614, and another Fort Orange in 1624, but in 1664 it was re-named in honour of the Duke of Albany – the future James II of England, and future James VII of Scotland.

Lachine Airfield in New Brunswick (New Brunswick is about as big as Ireland): Lachine was an RCAF (Royal Canadian Air Force) station to the west of Montreal and in 1941 became a transit point for supplies to the war in Europe. It is now known as Montreal – Pierre Elliott Trudeau International Airport.

Halifax in Nova Scotia is known as the "winter port" of Canada. In its magnificent harbour all the fleets of the world could anchor at once – "Jack's Reference Book". 1919

Nassau was burned by the Spanish in 1684 and then rebuilt by the Dutch in 1695 under William III of the House of Orange-Nassau. From 1703 to 1718 there was no governor in the colony and by 1713 the sparsely settled Bahamas had become a pirate haven. The Governor of Bermuda stated that there were over 1000 pirates in Nassau and that they far outnumbered the mere one hundred law-abiding inhabitants in the town. The pirates proclaimed Nassau a pirate republic, establishing themselves as "governors." Examples of pirates that used Nassau as their base are Charles Vane, Thomas Barrow, Benjamin Hornigold, Calico Jack Rackham, and the infamous Edward Teach, known as "Blackbeard", along with infamous female pirates such as Anne Bonny and Mary Read.

In 1718, the British sought to regain control of the islands and appointed Captain Woodes Rogers as Royal Governor. He successfully clamped down on the pirates, reformed the civil administration, and restored proper commerce. Rogers cleaned up Nassau and rebuilt the fort, often using his own wealth to try to overcome problems.

In 1776, during the American War of Independence, Nassau was invaded by US marines but after ransacking the place they only stayed for two more days. The Spanish recaptured it in 1782 but the British finally prevailed and it became part of the BWI – British West Indies. During the American Civil War Nassau was a staging and trading port for blockade runners who were supplying the Confederacy in their battle against the Union. More than a third of the ships used in blockade running were built or bought on the Clyde, many of them specifically for that purpose, and a good deal of the "rich runners" were Scots. After the civil war finished and after he was let out of prison, Jefferson Davis, the president of the Confederacy, actually came to stay for a while in Glasgow to see old friends and recuperate.

Foreword by Anthony Adolph

History is the study of anything and everything which has happened in the past, but it is only of any interest to us when it concerns us in some personal way. For a long time there has existed an artificial distinction between mainstream history and family history, as if the two genres were from different worlds, but in reality they are two halves of the same thing. Family history is what connects us to mainstream history. It is our route back, and the main reason why mainstream history interests us at all. The value of personal memoirs to both family and mainstream history is immense. Sometimes, when they are the work of famous people like Winston Churchill, they seem to tell us a great deal about how mainstream history was made in the first place. Most don't go that far, and often they seem to reflect more on the way individual people and families have been buffeted about by national and world events, than the other way around. Yet like the idea of a butterfly flapping its wings somewhere in the world and ultimately causing a hurricane somewhere else, it was the actions of each "ordinary" person, and the combined actions of every family, that caused so much of what mainstream history seeks to record and explain. Each of us, unwittingly, makes history all the time. So when the life of someone who has lived more in the thick of it than most, like Bill Leggate, is recorded in a book such as this, we should all be immensely grateful, for one of those flaps of a butterfly's wing is now a matter of permanent record. Bill has also included his wife Madge's story and so, in many ways, there are other butterflies also flapping their wings behind us all and changing and directing our lives.

I was delighted to be involved with the project by tracing the ancestries of Bill Leggate and by extension, that of his wife, Madge Leggate, nee Knight, and, as I showed with a famous sportsman in an episode of the TV series called "Who Do You Think You Are? ", where it turned out that the sportsman's great great great-grandfather was a poacher - you never know what you will find in family trees, however ordinary they might appear, until you start looking. I was particularly pleased to find a plausible route for the family back to seventeenth century Lanarkshire and to find that the Leggates are most likely descended from Adam Legate, whose job it was to render to the Scottish Exchequer the accounts of the baillies of Stirling in 1406 and who was, so to speak, a "legate".

Anthony Adolph, genealogist.

Family tree……………………………………Page 140

List of illustrations……………………………...Page 147

Picture gallery …………………………….Page 148

FROM PONY BOY TO PARADISE BEACH

Early days

These days, the job of pony boy on a ducal estate could only be described as "a job to move on from". It could never be seen as a real career either back then or now, but you've got to start somewhere, and whatever comes up you give it your best shot - especially if there's not much else on offer in the way of employment. You can always learn something and you may also meet some interesting people. Then, when the time's right, you move on, taking all these experiences and memories along with you.

August 11th 1922 was not the best of days for my mother, as it was the day when the stork paid a visit to deliver a handsome son, gross weight fourteen and a half pounds. After delivery the stork probably expressed his sympathy to my mother and flew off for his next assignment, hoping for a lighter task.

This arrival took place at 5 Stonehouse Road in Strathaven, Lanarkshire, at one o'clock in the afternoon of a hot day in high summer, I being the third child to be delivered to my parents (John and Jean) who were living with my grandfather John Leggate. My father was also called John Leggate, as was my elder brother. At this stage we were now six in a two room apartment. There was a bedroom, a living room and a kitchen. It might seem exceptionally crowded looking back from modern times, but it was not unusual in those far off days. Somehow, families squeezed in and managed. Overcrowding in this way had the benefit of ensuring that grown-up children flew the coop as soon as they were able. The living room had two built-in beds, a sink and an open fireplace with a swee, which is a swivelling metal bar for hanging pots over the fire. The "built in beds" might need some explaining, and when Samuel Johnson and his biographer, James Boswell, travelled through Scotland in 1773, they noted that: "Beds were often inside cupboards along the walls, much like enclosed bunks. Families packed into them at night, sleeping on lumpy pallets that were stuffed with anything from feathers to heather and straw. If visitors arrived, strangers though they might be (as Dr Johnson and Boswell found), they too were stuffed into these sleeping cupboards, sharing a bed with whoever was already there".

Our bedroom was grandad's alone. It was his domain and it was where he slept and kept his cage birds. He was an expert bird fancier and often showed at competitions all over Britain, even as far away as Crystal Palace in London. He was a keen member of Strathaven Ornithological Society and had also been a member of Strathaven Volunteers from 1887-1897. The Volunteers Rifle Company was made up of local men from all levels of society, who were armed and trained in defence and were getting ready for the Boer War offensive. In 1908 they became part of the newly formed Territorial Army.

My grandfather, John Leggate, was a tailor by trade, and he worked for Gavin Shearer Gents Outfitters and for others at various times. My great-grandfather, Robert Leggate, was a shoemaker at Sandknowe in the oldest part of Strathaven. Being a shoemaker, or a cobbler, was an honourable occupation in Scotland from the earliest times. Very often sons of cobblers became cobblers, generation after generation, like Alexander Selkirk, of Fife, for example, the famous seventh son of a seventh son, who, as I've said, came from a long line of cobblers, but wasn't satisfied with following the family trade. He ran away to sea, was shipwrecked, and became the basis for Daniel Defoe's world-famous story of Robinson Crusoe.

We lived in a handy place at that time, with so much going on within one hundred yards in each direction. First and foremost we had Gavler's or Avondale Castle on a bend of the Pomillon Burn. It was a playground for elder brother John and me; the main attraction was, of course, the artillery piece, a relic from the First World War, which we were able to scramble over and kid ourselves on. Added excitement was the legend of ghosts, as befitting all ancient ruins. The castle originally dated from around the mid-1300's and changed hands many times through war and peace. Its last owner was Anne, Duchess of Hamilton, who lived in it until her death in 1616, after which it gradually fell into disrepair. The Hamilton clan were the local lairds, but as a boy I had little idea that soon I would be working for the Duke. Our ghoulish natures were satisfied by a skeleton that had been found encased within the walls of the castle. Details on a notice board read: Around the year 1350, there was a castle in the middle of the small town of Strathaven. It was built by the Bairds on a bend of the Pomillon Burn. Then the Sinclairs took it over, and then the Earl of Douglas. The Earls of Douglas were suppressed by James II, and in 1455 it was taken over and rebuilt by Murdoch Stewart who was the illegitimate grandson of the Duke of Albany, and later became Lord Avondale. The castle passed to Sir James Hamilton in 1534, and changed hands once again in 1611 when it went to James the Marquis of Hamilton. The last occupant, Anne, Duchess of Hamilton, was apparently a red-haired firebrand of a woman who died in 1616. The castle was abandoned a year later. They became the stuff of folklore and legend.

According to tradition, the wife of a particular past lord so greatly displeased her husband that she was walled up alive in part of the castle wall. Nothing is recorded of her crime, yet it is said that she was led into a small purpose-built niche, blessed by a priest, given some food and water, and then walled up forever. Eventually, when a portion of the walls fell down in the middle, bones were discovered, giving some credence to this story.

Close by the castle at the heart of Strathaven, and spanning the little stream of Pomilion, is the Boo Backit Bridge. This late 18th century structure enjoys "listed status" of B category within the Strathaven Conservation Area. Children swam in the stream where it ran through meadows by the castle. Close by was also the town mill with its big water wheel whose rumble when it was working could be heard from some distance away. The mill was another magical place for a boy to let his imagination run riot. We'd roam down past the water wheel along the side of Pomillon past the sewage works, through the land of Findlay's Floors Farm and on down to where the Pomillon Burn joins the Avon river. In time, after much meandering, the Avon ended up in the mighty Clyde, but we, who were further upstream, had little connection with Glasgow and the wider world beyond our rural community; it was, after all, 20 miles away.

My father and mother, being busy with their work, were helped by my grandfather, who took us young ones walking. I particularly liked our walks along the railway lines. My grandfather, being such a naturalist, knew all the wild flowers, birds and birds' nests and could point out each one to his curious young charges. While we walked, grandad gathered plants which had seeds for his birds at home. There was little that missed his quick eye, but that was hardly surprising, since he had excellent vision, so good that he was a crack shot at a thousand yards at the shooting championships at Bisley. It was a great achievement. Bisley, in Surrey, was the home of the National Rifle Association, and in 1908 part of the Summer Olympics were held there. Beyond the castle and mill on Stonehouse Road on the left was the entrance to Strathaven Cemetery, and fifty yards further on was St Patrick Church. When I was a child the fact that my ancestors were buried in the graveyard meant little to me, but as I grew older, I developed a sense of pride, knowing that we were established in an ancient Scottish town, with our roots going back many centuries. Today, in the oldest part of the cemetery, there is a gravestone dated 1812, for two members of the Leggate ancestry. Also, scattered throughout the town, in several cemeteries, the remains of many Leggates can be found, with gravestones indicating different branches of our family. According to information received from an educated grandson of mine, the town has more Leggates per thousand head of population than any place in the world. It would be accurate to say that Strathaven is both the stronghold and cradle of the Scottish Leggates. However, in reality, the history of the family is rather complex and more details on our family name, in its various manifestations, are included later in this book.

My father, who was given the family name of John, but also known locally as Johnnie, served with the Royal Artillery in WW1. He had three brothers, and my uncle Robert won the Military Medal in that war. Uncle Duncan was in the infantry at sixteen years old and survived being buried by shell bursts to fight another day. Uncle Jimmy (too young for WW1) married and had a family. My father also had two sisters; Aunt Margaret and an Aunt Martha (Matt). Dallas was their maiden name and they lived at Burnt Island in Fife. On my mother's side were four generous aunts called Meg, Mary, Minnie, and Nan, who went off to America. My uncles were Walter, Dick, Jimmy, and another who died in WW1. My maternal grandfather, William Bennie (after whom I was named) was a miner by profession and, incredibly, spent some time in America as a fossil hunter. Exactly what he did out there I do not know, but when he returned to Kirkintilloch, to resume mining, he also set up a dairy-come-bakery which was run by my aunts Meg, Mary and Minnie. The three aunts made the shop a successful home bakery, and were internationally famous in their way because a lot of their products, especially at Christmas, were sent off across the globe to expats, gold miners in California and South Africa and tea planters in India, who wanted these things to remind them of home.

In 1927, when I was five years of age, my family moved to a new housing estate. We now had two bedrooms and a living room, kitchenette and bathroom. It certainly seemed very spacious after our previous cramped home. Grandfather had a nice hut built for his cage birds and tools and it sat at the top of our garden which was very steep. All the family took a great interest in the birds and at show times the show-cages were painted (black outside and a lovely green inside). When some were going to the shows we all trooped off carrying birds to the railway station for transportation all over the country.

My father was by now a postman and in those days a motorcycle and sidecar was his vehicle for the deliveries to the more outlying parts of the community. Around New Year time it would be amusing when he came home with the motorcycle and was unable to stand very well having had a celebratory dram at too many homes. Because he had been a cobbler prior to going to war, under our kitchen table was a big box with all his gear. He used solid materials, hard to handle even for a man with calloused hands, let alone a young lad like me. I was always up to a challenge and, anyway, I cherished spending time with my father. It's fair to say that he was a fairly taciturn man, but like most Scots, he could tell a good story. I learned some things about the legends of our neck of the woods, and some of the history of our family, but not really enough. Most of all, I developed a strong work ethic while sitting at that pine kitchen table, with my mother bustling about behind us at her never-ending chores.

Our mother Jean was a very good manager and also a good organiser, so we all had our allocation of jobs to keep everything spick and span in the home and garden. My own specialities were beating carpets, peeling potatoes, polishing brassware, polishing Dad's work boots and, assisting when any baking was being done. There were many other chores too numerous to mention but one of them included gathering horse manure for the roses and the rhubarb.

Living at Park Crescent was a kind of heaven on earth to all of us kids who had never really met before and on these new streets we were more than happy to indulge in endless types of games with new friends of all assorted ages. Summers were carefree and great fun. There was always plenty to do, most of which involved inventing our own entertainment, and the biggest thing in our young lives was the public park just at the foot of the road. It was only about two hundred yards away, and inside it was the Pomillon Burn, a magnet for us with its minnows, boulders and pools. Half a mile up the Pomillon was the Voe, a man-made dam which acted as a catchment for water which supplied the town's small industries, to drive their small workshop machinery in the joinery shops, and the mills for cotton and flax; it also acted as a reservoir for the town mill wheel. The dam also acted as the town's swimming pool and on good summer days and evenings there would be a fine turnout of swimmers and walkers on both sides of the water. It was generally used by experienced swimmers as it was quite deep, especially in the area of the sluice gate where it could be ten to twelve feet straight down to the bottom. As a boy, and once I could swim, I used to dive into the sluice when the dam was full until one day someone told my parents of my daring exploits and my dad came to the dam and caught me and whacked my backside with his slipper all the way home.

Further along from the Voe there was another popular and safer place where we young ones made a dam of rocks and stones that formed a good pool. It was only about two and a half feet deep but we could practice swimming until we were good enough and old enough to let off energy and we looked forward to testing our mettle in the dam.

Like many Scots, I enjoyed music. Social evenings often included singing and playing on various instruments. My father had once bought a couple of banjos from a market stall in Glasgow and eventually I was encouraged to pick one of them up and give it a go. Well, I managed to work with a plectrum (a pick) and to strum a bit of *Way Down upon the Swanee River*, but then, as someone who once listened to me playing after I'd told him that I was getting better at it observed: "better" was always going to be in front of me. However, it didn't deter me, and in time, I also tried my hand at the mandolin and the xylophone. Our lives were always full of activity, and not all of it was play. None of the families really had much money and so we all knew that we had to try to get some kind of a job or another that we could fit in with school. Part-time jobs were never seen as a chore or something to be moaned about. We earned some cash to help out. I spent many an hour with grandad mending shoes and boots to earn a few extra shillings for the home. In those days, we used real hide and leather and iron nails.

At eleven years old I had a paper round along with my elder brother John. We had to be out of bed by 6.30, and at the railway station at 7 am when the trains brought the papers to town. There were four paper boys in our shop, which was owned by a Miss Marshall who had a glass eye. Her assistant was a Miss Jenny Duncan who had a wooden leg. Between them they ran a well organised shop and were a joy to work for. The spring and summer of 1933 was wonderful. It was sunny and it felt great to be alive.

From the Glasgow Herald - May 24th 1933

There is every prospect, I learn to-day, that the 24 Italian flying boats, which are to attempt a formation flight across the Atlantic next month, will pass over Central Scotland on their ambitious journey. With Italo Balbo, the Italian Air Minister, in command, the two squadrons will fly on the first day from Orbetello, near Rome, to Amsterdam, and on the second day, probably June 11^{th,} the programme is to strike the English coast and then turn north in order to cross Scotland at its narrowest belt between the Forth and the Clyde en route for Loch Foyle (N.B. - in Londonderry N. Ireland, where it is spelt Lough Foyle). Arrangements are being made by the Royal Air Force for the reception of the flyers at Derry, where they will also be given an official welcome by Lord Londonderry, the Minister for Air.

The Glasgow Herald is perhaps where I read about it first. When it happened – in the July not the June, and their flight-path may have been slightly more to the south than in the Glasgow Herald's report - was when I experienced one of those moments that you often see in a film: a young boy is standing in the middle of a field, or he's out riding his bike, and he looks up into the sky, shields his eyes to see the plane overhead and is enthralled. This happened to me one day in July 1933. It was the day that aircraft really entered my life and an infusion of aviation fuel entered my bloodstream. To say that I remember it clearly is an understatement. Being a paper boy I had been reading the news on the previous few days about the formation - sometimes called an "armada" - of Savoia-Marchetti flying boats under the command of Air Marshall Italo Balbo – a very popular man over there and the Deputy "Duce" of Italy. The formation was flying from Orbetello just north of Rome in Italy and heading for the World's Fair in Chicago via Holland, Scotland, Iceland and thence via Labrador, Montreal in Canada and on down to Lake Michigan at Chicago. Orbetello was a military airfield but the flying boats could take off from the lagoon at Orbetello which had a surface area of almost 30 kilometres.

It was another of those clear sunny days and I was standing at the back garden door of our home in Park Crescent when I heard the drone of many engines and I went out and looked up to see these huge Italian flying boats that I knew were heading for America.

The intention of the Italians was propaganda - to show off the planes just like my grandfather showed off his caged birds – and to impress as many people as they could. I had known that these aircraft would be flying overhead near us on this particular day and I had hoped to see them. Later, I also read that they had lost one of the planes, and as I read the report that sad fact also went deep into my subconscious. There were to be other more personal heavy-heart moments of loss when pilots went down, but at that time, now over eighty years ago, this kind of event and flypast were just a tremendous achievement and a real feather in the Italian cap.

Some things you only realise later and it's usually in some quiet moment in your life, but that event was much more than a "road to Damascus" moment for me. It was almost a cathartic moment, a distilling of emotions. My interest in planes and just what it took to "keep the guys up in the skies", with its mixture of knowledge and technology and scraps of electricity and magic, began right there and then, eventually, inevitably, led to me signing up with the RAF.

Flying exploits were enormously popular at that time in 1933. Everybody was trying to out-do everybody else. Just a couple of months back, in April, the Marquis of Clydesdale - the future Duke of Hamilton – had led a stupendous air-expedition that flew over the top of Mount Everest. He had been the first to do it and in his Westland PV3 he'd pipped the French and German teams. It had been a very dangerous flight and that day the wind up there on the mountain had been 50% stronger than usual. However, Hamilton's second-in-command had been a McIntyre so he had some good Scots help.

I'm going to skip ahead in the narrative just for a moment here to tell you about the strange death of Italo Balbo. He was shot down in June 1940; killed by friendly fire as he came in to land at the harbour in Tobruk and just after a British raid had taken place. Balbo had made no secret of some of his feelings about the war for Italians, and the alliance with Germany, and so a lot of people believe he was assassinated.

One other thing: the airfield at Orbetello and, of course, its lagoon, was seized by American troops in June 1944 – including men who had been in Chicago that day in 1933, and applauded when Italo Balbo had landed on the lake all the way from Orbetello. The Americans turned it into a fighter base for P-47 Thunderbolts.

Two months before my fourteenth birthday I got a job during the school holidays as a temporary telegram boy. It was "full time", and it gave me a couple of months out on a bicycle for the first time in my life. I enjoyed it very much and the summer of 1936 was one of the best. I especially loved my journeys to the outlying farms to make deliveries, and when the job came to an end I got another on a fruit van for a week, and then another on a fish van which lasted up to the spring of 1937. I look back on all these small jobs that I did in my youth as being part of my training for my future life. I was always meeting many different people, learning about Strathaven, its workplaces, and how the town's people got on with their lives. I reckon it was all very educational. At fourteen I left school for good and began full time work, but I also attended night school four nights a week. The subjects I studied were English, Maths, Woodwork and Technical Drawing, and I also studied gymnastics. Our gym instructor was a very fine young man by the name of Billy Liddel, who was held in great respect by all who knew him. I had always kept fit with running, swimming and playing cricket, but these new formal sessions in the gym set me up for life and established a real love of keeping fit that in due course led me to amateur boxing.

My next move, and my first proper full-time job, was quite special to me. In many ways it was unique and I shall never forget it. In April 1937 I became 'pony boy' to the Duke of Hamilton at Dungavel House, which is about six miles from Strathaven on the road to Muirkirk. It was one of the many grand homes belonging to the Duke. The 13th Duke of Hamilton was a kindly old boy, although not really old in modern terms. He was disabled, semi-paralysed from an accident while serving in the Royal Navy. I was basically a servant at Dungavel but I was treated very well indeed. I have seen a lot of change, but nothing, absolutely nothing illustrates change to me more than the fact that beautiful Dungavel House is now called the Dungavel Immigration Removal Centre.

The name is self-explanatory. The house is policed by a force of security guards, but there are often real coppers outside. The house is surrounded by barbed wire and razor wire. It has gone from beautiful to ugly. On one recent weekend in August 2014 there was a national emergency at

Dungavel with a suspected case of Ebola virus which came with an African woman who was about to be deported. It was on the television news and there were pictures in the newspapers. I stared at them.

Often in my dreams I am cycling on the road to work. I'm back in the 1930's and it's a beautiful morning. My family were not well off but I happily bicycled to work every day from our home in Strathaven. My main job fitted the job title and description. I prepared the Duke's pony and the small carriage and got it all ready to take the Duke out for his daily airing. He was a lovely old boy, the Duke, but very disabled, and had to be lifted into the carriage by his male nurses. I had to be at the head of the pony at all times for the daily walk which took place along the main road or into the woods. Sometimes the Duke's "piper companion" walked beside the carriage and chatted to the Duke, and occasionally we would also be accompanied by dignitaries who might be at Dungavel for a visit. The piper was Pipe Major Matheson, a Hamilton man. Sometimes, on good Sunday mornings, there would be teams of cyclists on the road and it was a fine thing to see them all touch their caps as they rode on their merry way past the Duke.

That was on the daily "walk", our daily airing. Before we set off I had many other things to do. My first job of the day at Dungavel was to get out and about with a pail and shovel and gather up all the dog droppings on the lawns around the main house. Only then did I go down to what was called the aerodrome field to get the pony. His name was Bobby and I would get him up to the stables for grooming and I'd give him some oats while I cleaned the harness with saddle soap, and cleaned his brasses and whitened his collar. In short I got him ready for our smart little jaunt to wherever His Grace fancied going that day.

But before I hitch up Bobby once again and take a trot down Memory Lane, let me first tell you a little about Dungavel House itself and the estate. Dungavel was originally the Duke of Hamilton's hunting lodge. It was in the middle of a famous grouse moor but the family moved there semi-permanently after their magnificent Hamilton Palace began to subside due to the nearby coal workings. Although the palace was used as a naval hospital in WW1, it fell into neglect and had to be demolished in 1927. It had been built in 1695 on the site of an original 13th century tower and in its heyday it had been one of the grandest in the country and housed paintings by Rubens and Titian and Van Dyck. The dining room was so beautiful that it's on show at the Boston Museum of Fine Arts; but all things change. There is now an ASDA supermarket on the site of the old palace in Hamilton and Dungavel House which has also been a prison recently, is now an immigration remand centre with a new wing added lately to give it more capacity.

Today, television dramas, like the enormously popular series Downton Abbey - that are set in similar houses to Dungavel in the UK - are very popular all over the world, especially in the USA, and it's easy to see why. Apart from giving a taste of history, and of the auld country, and of "how things were" in those days in some levels of society, the house itself and its grounds and workings were a microcosm of society and like a community of its own. Not only like Upstairs Downstairs, another TV drama, with the gentry up, and the workers down, like in a big town house, but an estate and with the estate workers. Dungavel had just about everything that was required for the running of such a place in those pre-World War Two days.

It generated all its own electricity with a system looked after by a very competent electrical engineer by the name of David Quinn. The house staff consisted of seven or eight ladies of varying ages, who all had their different parts to play. There was the housekeeper, the laundry maid, the cook, and, of course, there were all the rooms to be looked after. There was also very nice accommodation provided for all who lived on the premises in order to be able to work there and to be on call. The butler had fine accommodations in one of the gate houses, while the gatekeeper was, naturally, in the gatehouse by the main gate. Beside the gymnasium and the stables were two garages and accommodation for two chauffeurs. The main garage usually had two or three Wolseley cars in it, all with different engine sizes, and the Duke's personal Rolls Royce which had a bed within so that the Duke could be transported in comfort between his homes.

I had a room next to the main garage for the pony harness with a large table to use when cleaning the harness and tack, but the small carriage itself, with its plush chair, was looked after by the head chauffeur. The gym was quite large and used mainly by the Duke's eldest son, the Marquis of Douglas and Clydesdale, whom I understood to be an amateur heavyweight boxing champion. There was also a second garage at the time which generally housed a shooting brake, and when the duchess was in residence there would also be her maroon Buick, an American saloon, a truly beautiful car.

The head gardener had his own accommodation within the grounds, along with the bothies, which were basic shelters or simple bunkhouses for the young gardeners. Also on the estate was housing accommodation for the families of the estate workers, many of whom worked in forestry, on the private roads, and maintaining the walls surrounding the estate. There was always plenty of upkeep on the numerous houses and estate lands to be done, and that kept quite a large staff very busy.

Like all big houses, Dungavel also had its own little chapel at the rear, and on the lawn on the south side was a swimming pool. One thing that always intrigued me was the lovely summer house, which was positioned to catch the sun and which could be rotated to make the most of the summer rays. It was quite the fashion in those days to have these small, rotating summer houses as well as rotating observatories where the aristocrats could observe the stars.

To the west of Dungavel on the opposite side of the Muirkirk road, there was a very large field where planes took off and landed, and at times there could be as many as three or four planes sitting all in a row. Beside this airfield was the gamekeeper's home and kennels, and this rural airfield was where Bobby, the Duke's pony, grazed for a time, accompanied by two large hunter horses which I befriended. The airfield dipped down onto the Drumclog road and in the mornings, on my way to get Bobby, the hunters would all be out of sight at the far end of the field which was lower than the top. So I started to trick them by carrying handfuls of oats in my overall pockets and standing at the top end of the field I would give a little whistle and they would all come running. When the oats were finished they always pushed me around trying to get into my pockets to see if there were more oats.

The person who "kept me right" at Dungavel House, and who kept me informed, was the head chauffeur, Mr Charlie Hughes. He was a very fine man with a lovely wife and two young children. Charlie did much more than just look after the cars. He was also the mechanic for the aircraft. Very likely he would have been some kind of ex-RAF man, or maybe even as far back as the Royal Flying Corps. He was a very good friend to me indeed.

Just like in any television drama series there were other characters, and one of them at Dungavel, and a man who played the biggest part in my life there, was a small gentleman called Monty Ames. Monty did various jobs at Dungavel and I thought he spoke like a cockney would speak but, at that time, I never knew for sure. He was very much the gentleman at all times and we got along well. One of his jobs was to prepare the big long table in the servants' dining room for lunch, where I also had a seat. I was taken under Monty's wing, and during my spare time in the morning, usually just before lunch, which was always taken at midday, I would help him prepare the meal and make sure that everything was on the table, like cutlery, condiments, water. When the time came to eat and the food was brought in with everyone in their place, the footmen – there were two of them called Mr. Peach and Mr. Rose - would serve the rest of us. For a young man like me it was always a lovely sight to behold the footmen wearing their official livery. Of course, the food was always cooked to perfection, thanks to a wonderful cook. Naturally, I didn't know much about the nuances of culinary perfection, but the servants' table at Dungavel was a wonderful place to find out.

The Duke and Duchess had four sons and two daughters as far as I could gather at the time. The names of their sons were as follows: Lords Douglas, George, Malcolm and David. The daughters were Ladies Margaret and Jean. When the school holidays arrived so did all the grandchildren. They all came to Dungavel for part of the holidays and during their stay I would have to prepare the pony a second time after the servants' midday meal. I would saddle him up so that the children could ride, but you had to watch out because Bobby was also a bit of a character. He had a mind of his own and sometimes if you approached him in the wrong way you might get a whack from one of his hind hoofs.

Part of the estate was the traditional Home Farm and Dungavel's was called Peel Hill. It was about three quarters of a mile away and the farmer, a very jovial man, as farmers are often depicted, made regular visits to Dungavel House with his produce. Almost everything the family ate, and the servants also for that matter, came from Home Farm: eggs, milk and cream, cheese, bacon and ham, meat and fowl, and fruit and vegetables in season. Needless to say, being so far to the north, the growing season was short and the diet was mostly on the plain and simple side although there were variations of plain and simple food at that time in Scotland. However, plain and simple at Dungavel House meant plenty of beef and mutton, served with root vegetables and greens like cabbages and kale. Although I never visited, apparently there were hothouses at Peel Hill and some luxuries were available like salads and some fruits.

Meanwhile, the year of 1937 rolled on and suddenly there was news around the house and estate that there was to be a wedding in the Duke's family at the end of the year. Naturally, and like in any TV drama script, this was something which caused a heady buzz amongst the staff. The forthcoming wedding was to be that of the Marquis, the eldest son, to Lady Elizabeth Percy - daughter of the Duke of Northumberland.

The ceremony was going to take place on the 27th October of that year in St. Giles Cathedral in Edinburgh with a thousand guests, and I remember the feeling I had when I was told I would be one of those guests. Yes, along with all the other staff I was invited to attend. Me! Attending such an event on a day that would go down in history! The pony boy at Dungavel House in attendance on the day that the Hamilton Clan ended their famous feud with the Percys - or vice versa. Anyway, I was bursting with pride.

The day came. We Hamilton Staff took our places on one side of the cathedral, and… yes, the Percy Staff took their places on the other. The marriage of the thirty year old Marquis of Douglas and Clydesdale, heir of the premier peer of Scotland, and of Lady Elizabeth Percy, sister of the Duke of Northumberland, would be a happy ending to a centuries old feud between the two historic families that had been immortalised in ballads like *Chevy Chase* and *Otter Burn*. One newspaper wrote:

"When congratulated on his engagement, which was announced this week, the Marquis said: "I've just returned from the most critical contest in my life. I started my quest at Alnwick Castle, Northumberland, and ended it successfully in the North of Scotland." The Marquis of Clydesdale, eldest son of the Duke of Hamilton and Brandon, is one of the most popular Britons in any walk of life. Long famous as one of the country's best amateur boxers, the Marquis earned the admiration of all by the heroic part he played in the memorable Mount Everest Air Expedition when he flew over the top of the unscaled mountain in 1933. Politics are

his main serious interest now; just as boxing is still his best sporting interest. So keen has he been on his political career for some years past, that after the Mount Everest flight, he refused a £2000 offer to go on a lecture tour in the United States. "I didn't think it was fair to my constituents," he said. One of the policemen on regular duty at the Members' entrance to the House of Commons was recently asked whom he thought the most constant attendant there apart from the Cabinet Ministers. 'Lord Clydesdale.' he replied. "He is always popping in and out, day or night." It was when Lord Clydesdale boxed for Oxford against Cambridge for three years in succession that he earned the title in sporting circles of 'The Boxing Marquis. In his boxing career he fought as many as six fights in one night. Lady Elizabeth Ivy Percy, elder daughter of the late Duke of Northumberland and the present Dowager Duchess, Mistress of the Robes, is 21 years old. One of the most travelled young women in Britain, Lady Elizabeth is keen on all sports. She was a train bearer to the Queen at the coronation".

The reception took place at the Assembly Halls in Edinburgh. I was a fifteen year old, rubbing shoulders with all the notables from throughout the land. On the day after the event the newspapers gave lists of all the various bottles of wine, and whisky and brandy. It all looked very impressive and quite possibly exaggerated although I would never know. It was a very exciting day for a pony boy.

The newlyweds went off on their honeymoon and to be honest I don't know where they went. I was a pony boy and knew little or nothing of wedding protocols and honeymoons, but when they arrived back home there was another reception. However, their arrival at Dungavel coincided with deep snow, and all the staff were waiting for them at the main gate with a horse drawn sledge with Bobby all harnessed up and ready to do the task.

Shortly after the newlyweds were settled in, a party was held at the riding school in Hamilton, which was part of the old Hamilton Palace. The occasion was to introduce the new bride to all the Dungavel House staff and to all the others who worked on other parts of the Hamilton Estate. Once again I had my invitation and enjoyed it very much. When the dancing was about to commence, an invitation was extended to the gentlemen that they could dance with the new Marchioness, if they so desired. I danced. I was fifteen and almost a gentleman. It was a lovely night.

The year 1937 was now coming to an end and Christmas arrived with all the staff going into the Big House one evening to have a party and to receive Christmas presents from the Duchess. I got a beautiful box of handkerchiefs. My job at Dungavel House was now also coming to an end. Looking back it was almost like waving farewell to the old world and to its old ways and courtesies; waving goodbye to the tail end of the sleigh as it rounds the corner with its riders and disappears into history. I was lucky to have seen it and to have played a small part, and sorry to leave, but being a pony boy is not really a trade in the modern world. It didn't pay much and yet it enriched me. I was an avid reader of newspapers that were full of the new, and I felt that I had to get out and on in the world and earn more money.

It's been seventy-five years and more since then and I still remember those happy and carefree times. I treasure the memories of all the people I met and worked with. I have always felt privileged to have had the experience of doing that kind of work. I believe it extended my knowledge in new fields.

From quite an early age - although I'm a Scot and football (soccer) is the best-loved Scottish game - my great sporting passion has always been cricket. There is a reason for this and, as so often, the reason is rooted in childhood. I think it was probably due to the fact that football – not just the best-loved sport but almost a religion in Scotland - was not allowed in the George Allen public park in Strathaven where we always played any games. Football was not allowed because George Allen had lost a son in an accident while the boy was playing the game and a so a small part at the top of the park was set aside just for cricket.

Well, we called it cricket, but we didn't have much of the proper equipment to play it with. However, little did I know that one day I would stand in an RAF uniform on parade at the world's GHQ and "temple" of the game, at Lords Cricket Ground in London. Meanwhile, back before the war, the basics, like the bat and ball and stumps for the wickets, were generally supplied by boys whose parents wanted to encourage their sons in the game. In fact, back in those days, although the real game required six wooden stumps about two feet high and standing in two sets of three – one set placed at each end of the twenty-two yard pitch, and with the bowlers bowling the ball at the batsmen from alternate ends - the shops like Woolworth's usually sold kits of only four stumps. This was perfect for a knock-up game on a family holiday and on a relatively flat beach with the single stump hammered into the ground at the bowler's end. Wherever you played, and we played in the park, the stumps at the batsmen's end were generally placed in the flattest piece of grass you could locate out there in the middle of your cricket ground to ensure that the regulation cricket ball bounced up and came-on to the batsman's bat from the bowler in as true and intentional flight as possible. However, cricket is a complex game and we couldn't afford to care too much for the many niceties and protocols or the evening would have turned to night before we ever got around to playing at all.

Our version was still a great game, though, and we played almost every evening that summer. Then, as we grew older, and became more proficient, some of us decided that we would form a team and try to put some money aside to buy equipment for the coming season. When the spring of 1938 arrived we had enough for us to venture into buying the basics for a whole team. We got bats and pads and wickets (the complete six stumps) and proper balls and the long bags to store it all in. We had entered the world of cricket and some of us even managed to afford white cricket trousers, or flannels known as "cricket whites". We did not, as some English wags joked, play the game dressed in white kilts.

There were about twenty-two of us youths involved (enough for two whole teams for a practice game) and all with an interest in the new club. We played under the direction of a very dedicated cricketer called Bill Galbraith, who kept us together and was an inspiration to us all. However, we didn't really get started because, after only one season, and just a few months with our smart new gear, it was September 1939 and we were at war.

Within no time at all about twenty of the lads received their call-up papers. My friend Charlie Ballantyne and I were both under age at the time for the call-up. I was seventeen, Charlie sixteen, but it wasn't long before I went off, and then later Charlie joined the Royal Highlanders. He was killed in the conflict and his name is up there on the Strathclyde war memorial.

But the real conflict and the real guns and bombs were still in the future and I became a member of our local YMCA which ran a gym night on Fridays. By the time I was seventeen and peace time ended for real, I was hooked on keeping fit. Apart from all the keep fit classes and gym, I was now working in the building trade every weekday and it was building up my muscles. I was often moving around great loads of timber for days at a time and thinking nothing of the labour. I was enjoying it.

On a Sunday our routine was to meet at the YMCA at 10 am for a service of one hour, and after that we broke up into various groups and passed the rest of the day in our chosen ways. A friend and I generally went walking in the countryside. On any given Sunday we might cover about twenty miles talking, debating, and putting the world to rights.

When WW2 got underway all my friends in all the groups at the YMCA would have many different experiences, and war puts you in strange situations. Sadly, after the war, we were never again to come together as the group we had been. We had grown up fast and for those of us who returned, life had changed so fundamentally that post war Britain was like a new world.

When I was seventeen, three weeks before the outbreak of the war, our family had moved to a far larger five roomed home in North Street. I had grown up in the cramped old place, and having more space for us all was very pleasant. By then, I was working on a new timber housing development and, with so many tradesmen going off to war, the younger lads had to tackle some of the jobs that were traditionally done by more experienced men. So we had to learn fast. I was still young, and I needed proper training, but I hoped that I could get taken on as an apprentice.

I continued my education at night school and, although the end of 1939 and the beginning of 1940 was called the Phoney War, Strathaven soon became a garrison town, with all the halls and cinemas and unused premises and such full of troops who were virtually camping out. I often felt that my home was an Army Depot. My parents and sisters would often bring home young men for a bite of supper. It was hard to get a seat at the table when I came home from work.

After the quiet phoney-period the country began to get seriously organised. We had woken up late to the danger and woken up unready, but now we were on the move and catching up. The real business of war and defence was beginning, and any able bodied young men, and older men who had fought in WW1, were asked to join the local defence volunteers, the LDV. We lads were ready and I think another mate of mine called Ian Cuthbertson and I were the first to reach the police station, where you could get signed on.

We were soon going through the initial training to get us knocked into shape so that we could back up the army if needs be. It was all very new to a seventeen year old recruit. However, at the other end of the spectrum, some of the older men, who had seen it all before, were enjoying the power of wearing stripes once again, but then, let's face it, we needed them badly. We needed their experience and their steady hand.

As time went on and the pressure of war increased, we in the LDV (the Local Defence Volunteers) set up roadblocks and manned them at night. We officiously stopped all the traffic and made sure there were no intruders about, and one of the most frequent men we stopped to check and search his car was Sir Harry Lauder, the iconic Scots music hall entertainer, who lived nearby on the outskirts of Strathaven and who just smiled when we stopped him and took it in his stride. In fact I'm sure he got some good material from it for his act.

My main memories of those times in the Volunteers was of playing cards in the rest periods between stints on roadblock duty, and then making our way home in the early mornings. Some of those late spring mornings were absolutely magnificent, with the sun just up and beautiful blue skies. It went some way to compensate for all the bother of doing guard duty.

The timber housing project turned out to be the biggest job I worked on, although when I started the scheme was almost completed. The outside of those houses were all "finished" externally with cedar weatherboarding, and most of them are still standing today, and they're still looking good. However, as soon as it was completed I was officially jobless; not for long, though. Even as I was registering at the Labour Exchange, one of the owners of a well-known company called J & C Fleming contacted the Exchange and asked for a youth to do a week's work at their joinery shop. One of their men had been taken ill. I just happened to be there at the right time and I was offered the chance. Fleming's had a joinery shop and a saw mill. My job for the week was to tend the furnace which was attached to the saw mill, and to burn up the surplus wood shavings made by the machinery.

After that week, on the next Monday morning, I went along as usual and sought out the boss. When he saw me he just nodded and said to carry on with my work. I instantly knew that this was my opportunity to become an apprentice joiner and being an apprentice at Fleming's was much sought after. Apart from being well-known, they were respected and you got a really thorough and comprehensive training. A lad could go from burning the wood shavings to helping the machine men, and then perhaps to work with them, while in between times doing loading and unloading work with the timber.

I worked hard to prove myself. I hoped to go from the saw mill to the joinery where I might be taken in hand by one of the fully qualified tradesmen. These men assembled doors and windows and painted anything that would be exposed to the elements. Another step was to go from workshop and small jobs on to the bigger jobs like housing schemes and building schools. It was all very interesting and promising. It was also a time when lots of qualified tradesmen had to leave their home towns and go into digs near their work to do a job. They were called journeymen and I met many of them and listened to them. A lot of them had fascinating stories. They talked easily of their experiences, their families, and the places they had lived in.

After a few months' work, and while still doing my bit with the LDV, changes were taking place in the building company which was doing less and less joinery, and more in the way of felling timber. My part in the new set up was to become a labourer helping to load the trucks with the cut timber, which I did. Unfortunately, the wages I continued to get were still those of an apprentice. The apprentice rate for labouring work was seventeen shillings a week, while the straight labouring rate for the same job paid a whole lot more.

It wasn't right. I was very disappointed with the unfairness and decided to move on. It was back to the Labour Exchange for me but the clerks there who dished out the jobs seemed to understand my plight and they soon offered me the chance to go on a course to learn to be an engineering fitter. It was a very good opportunity and I took it. This course was at a factory on the outskirts of Glasgow, with two different shifts, night and day. This meant that I would have to go into digs because travelling back and forth would be unrealistic.

Clydebank – 1941

The first house in Glasgow that I had digs in, along with three others on the course, was very nice and the landlady looked after us very well. Her husband was an engineer and at that time he was working on a new warship which was in the final stages of commissioning at Clydebank and about to be tested over the measured mile.

We had been on full air-raid alert for some time like all other major cities and ports in the UK, but the so-called Clydeside Blitz that occurred over the two nights of the thirteenth and fourteen of March 1941 was far worse than anyone could have ever imagined.

The main target was the John Brown Company shipyard but the warship that our landlady's husband was working on was far enough advanced in its preparation for sea to be fully armed and was able to do its duty in the protection of Clydebank – which was about nine miles from our digs. Unfortunately, during this time one of my companions in the digs started to go out of his mind and we had to restrain him till things quietened down. I had heard stories from the older guys in the LDV about men who had suffered mentally in WW1 from the incessant dropping of bombs or the nonstop artillery shelling and, suddenly, there I was, seeing it happen at first hand.

Later, we learned that four hundred German bombers or more had been on the raid and dropped a thousand bombs on Clydebank. Very little shipping had been damaged and the bombs had fallen mostly on people's homes. Out of twelve thousand dwellings that had been standing the day before, only seven thousand survived intact and many people were killed or injured.

The Hess affair. The Nazi Deputy Fuhrer heads for Dungavel in his plane

Some months later, on the night of 10th May, and as we made our way towards the training centre, the sound of a single aircraft became audible. We stopped, looked up, and cocked our ears to listen while at the same time getting prepared to duck into shelter. The plane had an unusual engine sound and we didn't know it at the time, but eventually learned that the aircraft was a Messerschmitt piloted by Rudolf Hess who was on a solo mission to meet, of all people, the Duke of Hamilton. This was an event that has gone down in history and many books have been written about it.

As I have said, my first proper job after I had left school in the late 1930's was pony boy for the Duke of Hamilton at nearby Dungavel House. The old Duke had died in 1940 and a year later Douglas had taken over the titles. Then, while I was away from home, one of the most bizarre events of the whole war happened almost in our backyard.

The Rudolf Hess affair was a very strange thing. Its echoes would reverberate around the world and even today those echoes continue to bounce around the walls of history. This is because the intricate plot can never be fully told or unravelled to the satisfaction of many sceptics and conspiracy theorists. However, these are the bare bones of what happened. On May 10th 1941, Rudolf Hess, Hitler's Deputy Fuhrer, climbed into his personal fighter plane and secretly flew over 1000 miles from Germany to Scotland in the belief that he was going to land on the airfield at Dungavel House, and then sit down with Douglas Hamilton - who would talk to Winston Churchill on Hess's behalf - and a peace deal between Germany and Britain could therefore be negotiated.

Many history buffs believe that this plan was all Hitler's idea and that he had sent Hess on the mission. Others believe that it was just Hess's idea alone. Whatever the truth, many believe that Hitler had simply had a panic attack. He had realised that with his upcoming blitzkrieg on Russia - on which he was about to embark in a matter of weeks to open an insane second front - and with the USA now making serious noises about entering the war - he had little chance of a cut and dried victory.

Whatever the idea was – and whether it was Hess's alone, or Hitler's alone, or Hitler & Hess's together - Rudolph Hess planned to meet Douglas Hamilton in order to tell him to tell Churchill that Hitler was offering Britain a deal - an olive branch.

But why did Hess pick out Douglas Hamilton to act as his intermediary? Well, according to some historians, an American journalist who went by the name of H.R. Knickerbocker (a man who had met both Hitler and Hess), had it on good authority that Rudolf Hess had taken advice from a friend named Albrecht Haushofer (a friend of Hess's who had supposedly also met Hamilton). The advice given to Hess was that Hamilton was known in pre-WW2 Britain as an appeaser. This meant that Hamilton had personally been against the war, and might still be in favour of a negotiated peace deal with Germany. Thus, Douglas Hamilton would be a good and well-placed man to approach in the first instance with the peace deal.

To say that Haushofer's advice was flawed and quite possibly very flimsy indeed, was an understatement, because it simply wasn't true. Douglas Hamilton was a man of great integrity. However, in the years preceding the war, he had travelled widely. He had been in Berlin and had met many of the German hierarchy.

Now, all this shallow and flimsy intelligence that appealed to Hess was compounded because in London there was another "journalist" – and this one was also a highflying American-born Conservative MP, named "Chips" Channon. The man was a social climber, but also a social diarist, and so he had a platform. Channon was married to a Guinness heiress, and he really was an appeaser. He was also a Parliamentary Private Secretary at the Foreign Office who hated the Russians with a vengeance and this often clouded his reasoning. Channon had also been in Berlin in August 1936 at a huge gala dinner and ball at the "Ministerium", along with all the top Nazis and other celebrity guests who included (as he happily wrote), "the Hamilton boys". Channon had written about this glittering ball in his social diary and, years later, when Hess landed in a field at David

McLean's Floors Farm - where my grandfather used to take us kids rambling and seed collecting - Hess blurted out that he had come to pow-wow with the Duke. *'Tell him I'm here,'* Hess had urged McLean as McLean stood over him with a pitchfork. *"Ich bin hier"* - as if that would sort out the confusion and give him a free pass.

Nevertheless, Hess's actions, arrogance, and temerity landed Hamilton in the pages of a scandal-hungry press - especially with the kind of newspapers that had no time for aristocrats, and for a while they gave Hamilton a hard time.

What had definitely happened was that Rudolf Hess had previously sent Douglas Hamilton a letter by a secret and circuitous route outlining his/Hitler's peace deal and suggesting a meeting on neutral territory in Lisbon, but the secret letter from Hess had never reached Douglas Hamilton because our own MI5 intercepted it. Our spymasters immediately saw it as a wonderful gift, a super opportunity to embarrass the Germans and score a massive propaganda coup that might help to get America into the war a bit faster.

However, the whole thing had to be handled right or the Americans would believe that Britain really was about to make a deal with the Nazis. Handled wrongly, the isolationists in America could conceivably use it to convince the rest of the country to stay out of the war in Europe. So it was a very delicate matter and, initially, it was fudged. MI5 dithered and corresponded back and forth with Hess for too long before Hamilton was summoned and let into the secret. By that time Hess was getting so nervous it's said that he made up his mind to forget all about meetings in Lisbon and fly direct to Dungavel.

So, there I am, one night in May 1941, away from home and on my usual way to the engineers' course with my mates when I hear a plane fly over overhead and I'm wondering what kind of plane it is. Then I'm wondering whether it was one of ours. Of course, and as I have done all my life and since I was a boy delivering the newspapers, I read them all and I followed the story, but that night on Clydeside, if had I been told what was happening, never in a million years would I have believed it - a plane piloted by the Deputy Fuhrer on his way to Dungavel House.

And, according to history, the story was even stranger: it seems that somewhere over Scotland Hess had become somewhat disoriented and he'd quite possibly lost the plot (it sounds a bit like a metaphor for the Nazis). He had looped the loop. He had flown upside down for a while. Apparently he had even blacked out for a while. He flew over the Scottish west coast, turned around and flew back inland. Then apparently he ran out of fuel, bailed out and hurt his ankle as he hit the deck. He then tried once again to become the high ranking German officer talking about peace deals, but in truth he had hurt his ankle and been captured by farmer McLean with his pitchfork. My grandfather would have loved the story - especially the bit about Hess subsequently becoming a jailbird.

Hess's mission had failed and in time the politically motivated smear campaign against Douglas Hamilton also failed. A few years later Hess found himself in the dock in Nuremberg where he was lucky to escape the hangman. He then became the sole inmate of Spandau Prison - an old castle in Cold War Berlin. He is said to have slowly gone crazy. A sole inmate guarded forever around the clock by a continuous rota of British, French, Americans and Russian soldiers, until he "hanged himself" on 17th August 1987, though nobody knows that for sure. Some of the old wags in Strathaven said they shouldn't have bothered with a trial and then sending him back to Germany, they should just have walled him up in our old castle.

However, Strathaven was now on the map. It used to be all castles and the clans knocking six bells out of each other, and then during WW2 it became ruined castles and hunting lodges and secret airfields, but it was a small town and it still is. Not too many famous people have come from here, but while we're on the subject I would like to tell you about Thomas Leiper. His story is interesting.

He was from Strathaven, in Lanarkshire. He became an American and then had to go to war with the old country. It's fair to say that he became one of the most powerful and influential men in early American business and politics. Born in December 1745 he left for Maryland at eighteen and became a genuine American hero after serving in what's called the American Revolutionary War. He had settled in Philadelphia and organised the First City Troop in the city which was then the capital. As one of their commanders he fought against the British in battles from Princetown to Brandywine to Yorktown, and helped retake Philadelphia after General Howe had taken it for the British in 1777. Leiper became a wealthy merchant who was also big in the tobacco business and president of the Common Council of Philadelphia. He was a democrat and director of banks of the city and of the United States. He also constructed the first working railway, albeit, initially, horse drawn. To say that he was well-connected or that he had been in at the start of "something big" would be understatements. He was close friends with the likes of Thomas Jefferson, and even rented him a house in Philadelphia when Jefferson was Secretary of State to George Washington. Some of his correspondence with Jefferson, who became president in 1801, was later published.

Leiper was the first influential voice to nominate another friend of his, called Andrew Jackson, for the presidency, which Jackson attained in 1829. Thomas Leiper forged much American history, and died at 79 years old in the July of 1825. He had married well, to Elizabeth Gray, when she was 16. She came from a strong political family and they had 13 children of whom 10 survived to adulthood. His subsequent family and descendants also married well, and they probably enjoyed rewards of land grants for fighting in the wars against the British and also against the Native Americans. Leiper had named his house in Wallingford, Pennsylvania, "Strathaven", and the estate itself is known as Avondale - both names being an obvious nod to his humble beginnings. I believe they are on what's called the National Register of Historic Places, and the house is said to be preserved complete with "fireproof vault". I'm told that many people visit the estate and take guided tours. The Leiper family has spread out from Strathaven right across the United States. There must definitely be some in Tennessee because just outside Nashville there is a town called Leiper's Fork.

Back in Scotland in 1941, I was being trained as an engineering fitter and it was fascinating. There were suddenly so many new tools to be mastered. I met trainees from all over. People who had perhaps excelled in their own chosen trade at home, but now had to train to do something different in wartime. We all had to learn fast. I have many memories of new friends that I made and two of them were of Italian extraction. Now Italy was already in the war on the Axis side, but so far, they had not specifically declared war on Britain. Quite how they worked that one out, I don't know, but initially there wasn't a problem with Scottish Italians.

However, when Italy got around to an official declaration on us, my friends started to come in for some abuse.

One of them was called George and his parents had a fish and chip shop in Glasgow where George would help out when he wasn't training with us. One night he found himself fighting a couple of men who had decided it was time to pick on him but George put both out for the count. However, he was charged and the court even fined him which was ridiculous. He might have had Italian parents but he was a true son of Glasgow.

Another piece of unpleasantness happened to George and me on the fitters' course. We were working away at a grindstone when two young men, who were totally unknown to us, approached and simply invited us to have a fight. We didn't want to get involved but they persisted and wouldn't go away so in the end we decided to sort it out - in the toilets. Sometimes it's simply a matter of *"come and have a go if you think you're hard enough",* and on arrival in the toilets we decided that George would take on the bigger of the two. So he told the guy to put up his fists but kept his own fists down by his side. Well, this threw the guy a bit but I kept watching him and he suddenly decided that George should hit him first. It was then, while I was also trying to keep one eye on the guy who I would fight, that I noticed George's opponent had a large file in the rule pocket of his overalls and I realised what was going to happen. So I took the initiative and jumped on him. I took away the file and George and I smacked him about a bit for his bother while the other guy just stood there and didn't say a word, and that was it. They never picked on us again, but some years later, when I was in the RAF and I had to go on another fitters' course, this time in Blackpool, I entered the common room of the boarding house where all the trainees were staying and there, right in front of me, was the Toilet Troublemaker himself. It was the very same guy from Glasgow, but this time he just gave me a quick look and a quick hello, and then he was gone. After that - and whether he was keeping a low profile or not, I don't know - I never saw him again. Maybe he applied for a transfer, but to this day it still amazes me how two people could demand a fight for no reason.

When my fitters' course in Glasgow had ended it seemed there was a shortage of the jobs that the courses were intended to fill, and so I said goodbye to my new mates and went home to Strathaven where I contacted my old employer, J & C Fleming and I was taken back on. I struck lucky because right then, Fleming had lots of work on their books, mainly sites for gun batteries and searchlight batteries and army camps. Most were of the Nissen hut variety, and in the Lanarkshire area, but one time a group of us were sent to work at an army camp a bit further afield in Dumfriesshire, on the Duke of Buccleuch's estate. We found accommodation in the village of Carronbridge near to the job. Housing around there consisted of mainly small cottages and beds were so scarce that we often had to sleep two to a bed. My bed mate was called Mr. Frew. He was older and very straight and organised and he sort of looked after me. He liked to go on long walks, which was good because I always found it hard to sit around and do nothing.

It was about this time that I was asked to volunteer for a new Government scheme that was being launched to take care of youngsters who were supposedly in danger of being at a loose end and therefore getting into trouble. I signed up at once. Being "at a loose end" was the polite and all-encompassing phrase that the government had come up with for rootless youngsters, often in cities, or maybe those whose fathers had joined up. With no paternal figure around the government was concerned that these youngsters might well get up to mischief. At that time there was no mention of kids being called juvenile delinquents. Anyway, the scheme would be overseen by the new Youth Welfare Organisation. I had never had time to be at a loose end in my life so far, and the idea was totally alien to me, but I was all for the new scheme. However, on the opening night in Strathaven, the guy who was to act as the new Youth Welfare Leader didn't show up and, despite my lack of experience in such work I was asked to take on the task. I enjoyed it, and in fact I did the job right up until the day I was called up by the RAF in March 1942.

Meanwhile, back at the army camp that I was working on, and which was nearing completion, there was a sudden influx of civilians who were a bit different from the rest of us. They were different, but not that much, given that many of our Scots ancestors were Vikings. These people were Norwegians who had previously lived in the area of Spitsbergen up inside the Arctic Circle. When our commandoes had mounted a raid up there against the Germans they had offered to take back to Britain any locals who cared to go.

Obviously the people had to make up their minds a bit sharpish but there had been quite a few takers, and now here they were, dressed as they must have been when the commandoes made their offer. They were from all walks of life. People that might make up a whole community in that part of the world, including as it turned out a cross-section of lawyers, police, clerks and some trappers still with white fox fur in their packs. Inevitably, those who were fit and ready for action against the invaders of their country were soon in army uniform. They looked good and, pumped up with typical "Eric Bloodaxe" type Viking spirit, they were raring to go. They were a real bonus to the commando raid.

Joining the RAF

I was also up for it and raring to go. A few months earlier I had volunteered for aircrew in the RAF but as time passed I presumed that nothing had come of my application. I wanted to become a pilot or an observer and presumed that I'd need a bit more formal education to achieve that goal. However, out of the blue, and while still in digs in Carronbridge, I received a summons to Dumfries, for a medical, prior to being called up in the RAF. I was now nineteen and a half. Oh, yes, I couldn't wait to get going.

My first RAF interview took place over two days in Edinburgh, and because I would have to spend the night in Edinburgh I was given a chit for a bed at the YMCA. As I stood in the queue I looked back along the line and saw this fellow waving to me and recognised an old friend from home. I waved back, booked in to the YMCA, and then stood by waiting for him to catch up and do the same. I said to him that I thought he was in the army commandoes. He smiled and nodded and then whispered that he was deserting and joining the RAF. This was because the army had been asked by the RAF if they had any men they could release who would like to work on radar. My mate had volunteered but then – a bit like me with my own application to join up – he had got fed up waiting for a transfer and so, here he was.

On that stay overnight in Edinburgh we decided to give the YMCA a miss. Instead, my friend took me to a row of houses in Edinburgh where all his commando mates were billeted. A while later I met him again when I was home on leave and I was eager to know how it had all turned out. He said it worked out fine. As soon as he had successfully joined the RAF he gave himself up to the MP's. There was a quick inquiry but, as expected, he was exonerated and got everybody's blessing that he was not a real deserter.

In the spring of 1942 I was finally accepted into the RAF. I left civilian life behind and was sent to Padgate, a small RAF station down near Warrington in Lancashire, for kitting out and medicals and jabs and everything else that I needed before being sent on for the tough square-bashing that would turn me into a real airman. I'll never forget something that happened at Padgate on the first day when we new recruits were all sitting around and taking it easy in our Nissen huts in between getting poked and jabbed and squeezed and interrogated. I was in the middle of a chat to a totally new acquaintance when he suddenly stopped and shouted across the hut to a Welshman to come over. "Hey, Taff," (all Welshmen are nicknamed Taff or Taffy just like all Scots are called Jock, and all the Irish are called Paddy.) "Come over here and sing a song for this Jock", and, more than willing to please, the fellow immediately came over, took a deep breath and burst into "Waltzing Mathilda", the famous Australian song. Australian the song might be – though the roots of the melody were probably here in the mother country – but he had a truly wonderful voice and everybody stopped to listen and enjoy the impromptu rendition.

In 1942, most people usually still lived where they were born or close by, but here we were, men from all over, rubbing along and all together in one hut. It was the perfect beginning to my RAF career.

From Padgate I went to Blackpool for the square-bashing and training. Blackpool was selected because of the huge amount of accommodation available there which in peacetime had always been filled by holidaymakers. Over the course of the war almost eight hundred thousand new recruits received their basic training in Blackpool. It was truly a great place to be trained. There was lots of sunshine, sea air, the famous beach and the Winter Gardens. We had plenty of freedom and I was soon in with a whole bunch of recruits to whom, just like me, a new world had opened up. It was also a time for learning about new things - like how to treat people properly; how to treat them with respect, and get along with them.

One day when we were being trained on the promenade I learned a valuable lesson in how to treat people and it's fair to say that it stayed with me for the rest of my life. Right in front of our squad our Flight Sergeant, who was a lovely man, was approached by the Warrant Officer in charge who, without preamble, began to deliver a pompous dressing down to the Flight Sergeant. Our man showed no emotion, did not argue or answer back, but then, when he was ready, he said simply but very firmly that he would be more than happy to speak with the officer, but… in his office later. I thought that our "Flight" had handled the situation and the ignorant W.O. perfectly and with superb expertise. I could tell from the reaction of the rest of the men that this was so. As I said, this lesson stayed with me all my life and occasionally I used his method in similar situations. On a lighter note, something else that has stuck in my mind all these years and perhaps not quite so important, were the lovely mugs of cocoa we had at the camp's baker's at midmorning breaks.

Oh, I really enjoyed my time in Blackpool and, with my *"at the double, lad,"* training finished, a new and now knocked-into-shape Bill Leggate in his smart new uniform was posted just a few miles away to RAF Squires Gate and No. 5 School of Technical Training for Air Mechanics. At Squires Gate I was taught how to be a Rigger Airframes/Flight Mechanic. This course, which before the war could last as much as six years - rather like an old-style apprenticeship - was now condensed into six months. Or, to put the new speeded-up version of the course another way, and as I was often told: *"there's a war on, you know, lad!"*

The famous Wellington Bombers were made at a huge factory close by which was run by Vickers Armstrong under Ministry of Aircraft Production. Over two and a half thousand Wellingtons were churned out there between 1940 and 1945. The course took in practically all the elements of an aeroplane's workings apart from the engines. As in many RAF establishments a large number of the instructors were civilians. I was hearing all sorts of voices and accents and it was just like learning a foreign language where you have to tune-in and listen carefully to pick it up. This also improves your overall concentration. There were times when I heard a voice and I turned around expecting to see Mr. Charlie Hughes, the head chauffeur from Dungavel House, who had also been the Duke's aircraft mechanic, but I never did, and I would smile to myself at the "echoes of Dungavel", and quickly get back to what I was doing. Most training took place in a huge hangar that was fitted out with all the requirements and included vintage aircraft like the Fairey "Battle" and Hawker biplanes. The Hawkers were now redundant but were put to good use to show us the basics of construction and their component parts. I was now an RAF man and I loved the lectures on the Theory of Flight. It took me over and soon became, not so much an entirely new interest in my life, but more like a completely new life. Before I went on any of these technical courses, and apart from the aircraft at Dungavel and the Italian flying boat flypast, and a "Flying Flea" with a motorcycle engine piloted by a Frenchman at a beach at Ayr, I had only seen pictures of aircraft.

I had already known some really good summers in my short life but the weather in that year of 1942, while I was on both my basic training at Blackpool and on the riggers course in Squires Gate was historic. We had the sea, the beach and some proper facilities for sports and recreation. With the course finished I got a short period of leave back home and then it was off to the famous RAF Duxford to join the AFDU – the Air Fighter Development Unit. I knew that Lady Luck was now on my side because this posting was one of the most interesting that an airman could ever get. On the journey I had to change from the train to a bus which went from Cambridge railway station. It was still early morning and the bus hadn't yet arrived when I met a couple of other airmen who were just coming off guard duty and they took me off to a canteen they knew. I thought I recognised one of the men and when I asked him where he came from it turned out that he had been to school in Strathaven where his dad was a police sergeant. That kind of chance meeting happened to me all the time during the war, so it must have happened to everybody. People from all walks of life were thrown into a general melting pot. New friends were made, sometimes for life, sometimes for a short while.

As I write, all these years on now, I can still remember that early morning. We were still in time for breakfast and as we made our way to the canteen we heard a plane above us and then all of a sudden a loud bang. The plane had been a Typhoon, nicknamed a "Tiffy", and it had been part of a new squadron being formed at Duxford. It had crashed on the airfield and later I heard that it was suspected the pilot had blacked out when doing a tight turn. This was my introduction to my first day at Duxford. It wasn't the first time that such a thing had happened, and it was not to be the last.

After breakfast I went off on the bus and found my accommodation and then headed for the airfield itself. I located the unit to which I had been assigned and made myself known to the officers, who told me what my duties would be: the main business of the unit, amongst many other things, was to test the latest modifications on fighter aircraft. By lunchtime I had a fair idea of what I would be doing and learning and what the unit was all about. Teatime came around and I had still not met any of my new billet mates. Then one of them came up to me and chatted a bit and during the conversation he said he was going to a dance in Duxford Village that evening. Why didn't I come along?

I agreed to go and with him leading the way we took one of the usual camp-shortcuts under the perimeter wire and on to the village hall. We paid our entrance money and in we went. Then it all happened very fast. My new friend was straight out on the floor and dancing with a girl, and then he danced straight into a brawl. Seconds before this happened I had only just plucked up my courage to do the same – apart from the brawl, that is. I was only halfway around the floor with my partner on my very first dance when a commotion got up. I took one look in the direction of my friend which of course turned out to be exactly where all the commotion was happening. He was involved in a fight and getting the worst of it from a big corporal.

I quickly excused myself from my partner, went over to the rumpus and picked up the big corporal from behind with my arms. I carried him out of the hall and dumped him out on the steps. I can't remember too much else about the evening after that but I think it was relatively peaceful after the rowdy start. I remember making it back through the break in the perimeter fence and back to my billet. However, what I do remember quite clearly is that as soon as I was in bed and had just dozed off there was another commotion and I woke up with a start. There in the room, bold as brass, and steamed up with boozy indignation, was the very same corporal along with some of his other drunken cronies and it was obvious they were on the hunt for my hapless friend in order to give him the rest of the pasting, and maybe me, too, for interfering. When I sat up and got ready for the expected onslaught they quickly came over and whispered a drunken reassurance that I was not an intended target before they continued to search the room but they didn't find him because he was under my bed and they weren't going to come too close to me again.

Eventually they departed and the poor guy crawled out shaking from under my bed and stood there watching the door. I shook my head as he thanked me and I thought: what a way to join a new unit. Of course, and as usual, it turned out that the corporal was the camp bully. What stuck in my mind later was the thought that, just like the bully in the scuffle in the toilets, I had never met any of those men before, and I never saw them again, either, not even the corporal.

The planes based at Duxford AFDU were a mix of daytime and night fighters and bombers. My job, along with many other technicians, was to service them, and I got to see the rarities at close hand. The Spitfires and Hurricanes became very well known, of course. They were the heroes of the Battle of Britain, soon to be iconic, and their dog fights over the Channel and Southern England were later set to valiant music by the likes of William Walton in many war films. Rightly so, but we also had many others planes that played a big part: like the Defiants, and Lysanders, and Bell P39 Airacobras, Typhoons, Mustangs, Walruses, Clipped Wing Spits, Hudsons, Lightnings, Lockhead Venturas, Mitchells, Beaufighters (the Beau), Mosquitoes, Marauders, Bostons and Ansons.

All in all it was a remarkable collection of some of the greatest planes ever flown, most of which were hardly ever heard about in the years after the war. There was also an interesting flight of planes that the airmen called The Flying Circus. These were a number of captured German planes which were then tried and tested to find out their secrets, and those secrets were used to our advantage. Sadly I never had the privilege of a close-up look. It has to be admitted that, scientifically and technically, the Germans were always very advanced. We only have to consider their early expertise in rocketry and the genius of men like Wernher von Braun, who the Americans secretly recruited and spirited off to the USA at the end of the war to form the basis of what would eventually be called NASA. Technically the Germans were good and in some areas they stood out.

To illustrate this I'll tell a funny story I learned from a younger friend of mine. It concerns the famous Berlin Philharmonic Orchestra. Apparently there was an American soldier, an officer who loved classical music, and when he was stationed over here he used to work at night at one of our British airfields. He liked to tune into their live concerts beamed from Germany, although tuning in to German stations was generally frowned upon. This officer suddenly realised one night that, not only was the sound quality quite superb, but the orchestra had been playing continuously for about three days straight without a break. How? It was common knowledge that the Germans often supplied their frontline armed forces with pep pills like Benzedrine, but to the Berlin Philharmonic? Surely not! However, he began to investigate, and he found out that the Germans had invented the tape recorder. That was how the orchestra was able to play for days on end because they were recordings. The early models were very cumbersome but the Gestapo had got very interested.

Directly after the war, and in very proper pursuit of this innovative technology, a military search party was sent to Germany which included not only various boffins but technical staff from EMI's famous recording studio (now called Abbey Road). Back then, as now, it was located in St. John's Wood, London, but even after the war they were still recording directly with a needle straight onto wax discs; not for long though. The Americans were also in Germany on the prowl to find these new tape recorders, and one of the early investors into this new technology was none other than Bing Crosby. Bing quickly worked out that with tape he could be in several places at the same time and earn several loads of money.

Rather like a reception area of a large hotel with guests checking in and out, flying routine at Duxford was based around Dispersals. After their morning tea the pilots and crews would be collected in trucks that drove them out to the runway where the planes were being prepared by fitters and riggers - of which I was one. It was all very busy and exciting with all the coming and going. You felt that you were totally involved, and you had to be on your toes and mentally alert. Tanks were filled with high octane fuel and armourers would be ensuring that weapons were loaded correctly and ready for action.

Breakfast was eaten in rotas in huts which were always within sprinting distance of the runway. Out on the airfield there was always the difference between the buzz of activity from technicians, mixed with the inactivity of air crews ready and waiting to fly off and fight. It was normal on sunny days to see pilots and crews in deck chairs reading books or magazines, as if they hadn't a care in the world.

However, there was always an underlying tension. At dispersals it was normal for there to be long periods of quiet and then sudden incidents. There would be days, weeks, when everything would be working fine and then all manner of things would happen at once. At that time at Duxford the runway was grass and one day six Spitfires were in a line facing the runway when another Spit came along to do a take-off and his wing tip struck three of the parked aircraft. At the same time another Spit had just taken off but his engine cut out at about a thousand feet so he just turned it around towards the runway and… he glided back in. Then, as we watched, and with all the bells and fire-fighters trucks bouncing off and milling around his plane he just got out as though nothing had happened, went over and began to carefully stroll up and down the line inspecting the three damaged aircraft. It probably took his mind off his recent brush with mortality.

Everyone at Duxford was very curious about a particular fighter ace who dropped in from time to time. He was a Brit by the name of James MacLachlan and he was a legend. He was known as *One-armed Mac* because he had lost an arm in combat over Malta while flying a Mustang. His opponent that day had been another great ace named Herr Oberleutnant Joachim Muncheberg. The German ace had won a string of medals, including two Iron Crosses and the Cross in Gold, during a career of some five hundred combat missions in which he shot down one hundred and thirty-five Allied aircraft, including Spitfires and Hurricanes on the Western Front, and Russian MIGs in the East. He was shot down and killed in March 1943, aged twenty-three.

Mac had been fitted with a prosthetic arm and continued to fly with his usual jaunty bravado, joining the ranks of other veterans who had lost limbs like Douglas Bader, and who often refused to admit they were disabled in any way. After a career during which he had been awarded the DSO, the DFC with two bars and the Czechoslovakian War Cross, Mac was shot down by ground fire over the French coast in July 1943. He was also twenty-three years old. That was one of the sad things about the war; that the casualties were so young.

That summer, while at Duxford, I turned twenty years of age and one day, after about three months at AFDU, I had a bit of a close call myself. I was being sent on attachment from Duxford to another unit called Fighter Affiliation Unit, FAU. This particular unit comprised three Spitfires and crews and a crew of mechanics to maintain them. The purpose of the unit was to visit bomber squadrons in the Lincolnshire area and use the Spits to teach bomber pilots how to take evasive action whilst among enemy fighters in battle. A pilot was detailed to fly me to my destination and the two of us were in a Boeing B25 Mitchell bomber. It was my first time aloft and I was equipped with work kit (a tool box) and parachute.

We took off, but at about a thousand feet one of the engines packed up. While the pilot turned back to base he told me that as we had a full payload of fuel we needed to lighten up and jettison some gear. So out went my tool box which weighed about a ton. Even now I often wonder where it landed and hope that no damage was done. I always hoped that nobody got flattened and that perhaps someone found it and made really good use of the contents. Maybe it changed someone's life, - who knows? But back then I had to work out how to ditch my parachute which wasn't easy because I'd never made a jump and I must have pulled the rip cord by mistake and suddenly there was parachute everywhere.

While I was still untangling myself we landed safely, but there was no hanging around. I just picked up another new tool box from the stores where I got a funny look from the guy in charge - although he didn't ask and I didn't offer - and then I set off again, this time in a Boston bomber. So, in short order I was now on my second flight, almost a veteran, almost an old hand.

The "Flying Squad", FAU, was a mobile unit, and while we weren't exactly overworked, being on the move was different from being in a stable environment. After a while our clothes were very much the worse for wear and badly needed replenishing, but we were never in one place long enough to be outfitted with new garments. Some of our chaps started to grumble about the shabby state we were always in. I couldn't blame them because we looked like a bunch of travelling tramps looking for the soup kitchen. It's fair to say that it was so bad that all we needed was a couple of bottles of Buckfast Abbey tonic wine (Buckie) in brown paper bags and we could have been checking-in at St. Mungo's.

By the time we got to RAF Swinderby in the flat lands of Lincolnshire, the grumbles had turned to loud moaning. We were allocated a Nissen hut and as we started to unload all our gear I decided I would sort it out for everybody, right then and there. Like an actor waiting for his cue, I had my props ready. It was a box full of gear that was destined for the office where our officer in charge, Flight Lt. Deveral, would be sitting behind a desk. I marched "on stage", and went up to his desk where I did a smart turn and bent over so just my backside was facing him.

He was a good man and I sensed that he wouldn't take my play-acting as insubordination. He got the point immediately. Then he sat back in his chair as far as it would go – an early lesson for me in what's now called body language - and said, "Good Lord, man. Is that all you've got to wear?"

"Aye, it is, sir!" Well, thankfully, in no time at all we were all kitted out to our requirements. Walking around like tramps had been bad for morale. However, then something equally rotten happened. When I was recalled from the detachment to Duxford in order to be posted onwards to Grangemouth in Scotland and a Spitfire Operational Training Unit (OTU), embarrassingly, I was held up at Duxford for a few days because I had caught scabies. This was probably because, like many of us who lived in crowded old huts, we were constantly on the move before we could get our clothes laundered, or get some new stuff to replace our worn out tat. It was awful. The only treatment at that time was a severe scrubbing all over with a hard brush and carbolic soap. So, red, raw, moving slowly and carefully, but pronounced scabies-free, I was finally fit to move on.

Grangemouth – 1942

It was not a large airfield. Its main job at that time was training new young pilots about operational skills on Spitfires. I became one of the team who serviced the aircraft, saw them off, and looked after them on their return to the blast bays for attention before their next outing.

The airfield was near Falkirk which at that time had a population of about a hundred and fifty thousand people and so suddenly there were all the facilities of a big town for any available spare time. Like all places where there are a lot of people there was activity, laughter, and high jinks as well as the more serious things.

Not all the mechanics were men. There were women, too, who did as good a job as any man. Overall, the camaraderie and the almost instant friendships that we formed during those war years became stronger much quicker than usual. I remember one Yorkshire fellow named George, and I have to say that he did look straight off the farm but, as always, looks can be deceptive.

One day his task was to check out the engine of a Spitfire which had just come in from the workshop after a major overhaul. George did his tests and reported to his superior that he was dissatisfied and recommended that the cylinder head should be taken off. Maybe he was hearing the wrong sounds. I don't know. It was certainly a good thing to have a finely tuned pair of ears. Anyway, the head was taken off and lo and behold there was a feeler gauge which had been left inside the engine by another mechanic. George had learned his trade well and probably saved the life of a pilot.

Learning to fly, especially in the very fast Spitfires, was a dangerous occupation in itself, and almost as hazardous at times as the combat missions that, came along as soon as you'd got the hang of it. One day an instructor arrived at the dispersal area with two young Canadian pilots to carry out a training exercise. The Instructor was called Lt. Doll, and he was someone I already had some acquaintance with. He was a tall man. He had the air of a buccaneer and always had a sheath knife stuck inside one of his flying boots. We got their planes started up and away they went off up into the blue. About an hour later Lt. Doll arrived back alone. He said that the two pilots had touched wings and gone down fast. I relived every moment of that day in detail in 2010 when I saw a report in the paper about a memorial being erected to those Canadian boys.

RAF Squires Gate, Blackpool – 1943

I had learned a lot at Grangemouth about life and death and about trusting your instincts. As usual I had met many fine people who I then had to leave behind because I was off on another course on aircraft and engineering. The new course was back at Squires Gate near Blackpool and as usual I got a little bit of home leave and then boarded the train back South. It was an upgrading course, in official terms Fitter 2A Airframes. The course and the new accommodation at Blackpool provided me with a complete new set of good friends and mates. As usual they came from all over Britain and all over the world and there are some good stories.

The first airman I made contact with was a Geordie from Newcastle. I had only been there a few days and hadn't really got to know any of the others so far when he came up to me and started chatting. George Tilley was his name. His father was a wrestler and George himself had been training to be an Olympic runner before being called up. He told me that he was still trying to keep up with his training by running along the seafront starting at 06.00 hours, but he said that the training was much easier with a bit of company and he asked if I would care to join him. Well, I had done some different sports in my life but straight running hadn't been one of them, but I said that I would give it a try. So we started what I called "this running lark", and being totally new to this kind of serious exertion I went through a lot of agony before I got any pleasure from my efforts. It was also the beginning of a wonderful friendship with George which lasted the whole of the course. We became known as The Runners and I ended up as fit as a fiddle. We ran miles along the seafront and along the sands, too.

I must also tell you about Bob, who was my room-mate at the digs during the course when I used to go off running with George. I suppose Bob was a solitary kind of fellow. Tough looking and so well-built that at times he reminded me of the comic strip character Desperate Dan. We got on very well. He liked a quiet life, kept no company that I knew of, enjoyed a quiet pint most evenings and that was about it. One night after having his pint he was on his way back to the digs when he passed a pub on the seafront where two men were handing out a rough time to an older gent. Bob came upon this scene, and almost as a matter of course, put both of them out for the count. Then he checked up on the old guy and continued on his way home.

When Bob mentioned this to me my first thought was that the two bullies must have wondered what had hit them. Bob told me that he was a member of the Kilmarnock boxing fraternity. At the time I just thought to myself that he was probably a handy friend to have in times of need, and I thought no more about it, but deep down inside I think I fancied myself as a boxer because the first chance I got to participate, I signed up.

And in the meanwhile, I think maybe my attitude was changing a little bit. Besides being super fit, maybe there was lots of adrenaline running around my system, too. I really don't know, but I was definitely what they call these days "pumped up". On the course at Squires Gate we were bussed to and from our digs, also at lunchtime and always with a sergeant in charge. Well, one day after lunch we gathered to be taken back. The bus duly arrived and the sergeant called us to order to be ready to board. However, he took one look at me and, for some reason, told me to wipe that smile off my face or he would wipe it off himself. Without thinking, I immediately replied that it would be fine, *"anytime you like, Sergeant."*

Now, maybe Bob overheard this exchange, I don't know, but as for the Sergeant he looked a bit stunned. He didn't say anything and I think he must have taken my insubordination reasonably well because it went no further. However, I decided that in the future I would be more careful in what I said, and not so quick to lose my temper, although at times it wasn't easy, and at my next posting I found an outlet for some of my excess energy and adrenaline, or maybe I should say that it found me.

As usual the course was coming to an end and we all had to go our separate ways. George went off to India, and I went off to the less exotic R.A.F Henlow. I got a lovely letter from him one day thanking me for providing companionship, and friendship. He said it was something that he would always remember, and so would I.

RAF Henlow – 1943/44

Another course had finished and I found myself on my solitary way to 13 MU (Maintenance Unit), in Bedfordshire. It was a big permanent station situated just inside the camp. At RAF Henlow you could get direct trains to London, and being a permanent camp it had a good number of facilities. It had a gymnasium, and as I loved to work out this was a big bonus for me. That was when a boxing instructor saw me working out and proposed that I should become part of the team. As I've said, and although I couldn't put my finger on it, I probably needed an outlet for all the steam I was continually building up, and that needed to be let off every day. After my six months of Olympic-style running at Blackpool with George, I must have looked the part to the instructor. So I agreed. Even though I had never had the gloves on in my life I immediately told him I'd have a go and he issued me with a starter kit consisting of mitts and a leather skipping rope.

Unfortunately, that was as far as the kit went, there was no instruction manual and so initially I got very little guidance and instruction in the finer points of the fight game. Nevertheless, I began to enjoy it and I began to learn. Boxing is something you have to learn quickly otherwise getting in the ring is the daily equivalent of being beaten up. The boxing instructor went by the name of Harry 'Boy' Charman. During his career he had gone fifteen rounds with Jack "Kid" Berg - a world junior welterweight champion back in the 1930s. Also, being a London boxer of some repute, Charman knew some of the big names in the game. At Henlow he was a Sergeant P.T.I. (physical training instructor) but easy to get on with - not a bully like some of them. Occasionally, he would want to get in the ring with someone to get a bit of exercise and having picked up a bit of skill I sometimes used to overdo it and give him a bit of a rough time. I would show off and smack him about. Of course, one day I must have been a bit rougher than he cared for and he soon let me know that if I kept it up he would give me a "doing-up". For my part, and with the adrenaline running, I gave him a return impression that if he made the wrong move I'd give him a bit more. However, we both backed off and came to a level of understanding with each other.

Harry was a good man and I learned that after the war, in the 1950's, he fetched up in Fiji of all places, where he became a real local hero by training the very first Fiji Islands Olympic boxing team for when the games took place in Melbourne, Australia – which, given that the Fiji authorities probably didn't have two pennies to rub together, wasn't too far to travel. I don't think they won much in the way of medals but they certainly won a lot of fans and admirers and by all accounts acquitted themselves well. I never did learn how Harry had come to be out there in Fiji in the first place, but I did read that he had set up a gymnasium with the idea of keeping the local street lads out of mischief. He had called the gym *Charman's All Races Gymnasium,* so maybe that's a clue.

Meanwhile, back during the war in Henlow, and with Harry Boy instructing, I was soon having a few bouts as a novice. The venues were hardly Madison Square Gardens - one was at Hitchin and one at Acton Town Hall. Other bouts were mainly back at the camp at Henlow. I must also admit that, as far as my RAF Henlow boxing CV is concerned, I received more second prizes than firsts. Still, meeting all those other novice boxers in the team taught me some things. It taught me that using sport or exercise to let off steam is a very good thing. Maybe not boxing, but young men need an outlet of some kind. Another thing I learned was that we should consider the qualities of others. Nothing is ever as it seems at first glance.

Another fellow I met up with at the bigger boxing occasions was the man who officiated at them - the announcer. This was the guy who introduced you, and called out your name. He was a lovely man and his name was Patsy Hagen. Now Patsy was one of those guys who are gifted with a sports-announcer's voice that sometimes becomes part of the fabric of life. They become instantly recognisable. In those days radio was king, boxing was big, and the announcer's voice was always a great big part of the show. Patsy was the eyes of the folks at home and in the pubs all around the country who never got to see the fights. They were entertainment. He was like a fairground barker. He would have been the barker at the Coliseum in ancient Rome. In the ring he would whip up the crowd and say *"And in the red corner…"*

From Pony Boy to Paradise Beach

Now, I had heard that in peacetime Patsy was a railwayman who somehow became an announcer at some of the big boxing events broadcast on the radio. I don't wish to trivialise but I've often wondered – as, of course, you sometimes do - if Patsy had started out by announcing the trains and he was so good at it that some boxing promoter heard his voice at the railway station one day when his train was late and tracked him down and signed him up. Probably not, but you never know. Nothing is ever as it seems at first glance, and what I do know is that Patsy became so famous as an announcer that after the war he even appeared in *The Goon Show* on BBC radio. The Goons with Peter Sellers and Spike Milligan and the other comics were so famous in the 1950's that for many people – including the Beatles who were growing up at the time, and especially for John Lennon – the Goons were on the *"not to be missed"* list.

Patsy appeared in a typical episode called *The Terrible Revenge of Fred Fumanchu,* where he more or less played himself and announced his lines like: *"And on my right, representing the empire and wearing a kilt, a shamrock, four leeks, a thistle, and a turban made out of a Union Jack, is Major Dennis Bloodnok - an Englishman."*

Being in the boxing team at Henlow brought certain little privileges, like having a pass, a chit of paper that allowed you to stop work earlier than the others and to have an earlier tea before going to the gym. Of course, when an event was on, there was also a good supper for all involved. At Henlow, as usual on any big base, there were airmen from all over the world and one mechanic I met was a guy from Rhodesia – nowadays called Zimbabwe. I had heard all about him before I met him. He was a studious type who was very fond of poetry which he used to read aloud in a very educated voice and people gathered to listen. In those days before TV you took whatever entertainment you could get. Eventually, I made his acquaintance, and he told me a very strange tale:

What happened was that I had asked him straight out what such an obviously well-educated man like him was doing as a mechanic in the RAF. I suppose, being an educated man, that he could have quoted the story of Lawrence of Arabia back at me – about when Lawrence had joined the RAF as a lowly mechanic under an assumed name. Maybe he didn't know that one – and at the time I definitely didn't know it, either - and so he related his own story, or what he called his downfall.

Apparently he had trained as a pilot in Rhodesia and had reached the point of flying solo. However - and it's probably another example of young men with their egos and their hormone levels running very high - it seems that novice pilots out there used to buzz the local village and see the poor black villagers run for cover. This was some kind of weird rite of passage, and he had decided that he must keep up the tradition and be just like the others. Except that when he tried it a young woman who had probably had enough of their "roaring boy" antics stood her ground, defiantly waited for the plane to come hurtling in low, took aim, and then hurled a rock which shattered his propeller. It was a good shot and he didn't blame her but said he was lucky not to be killed. However, that's where his luck ran out and the tomfoolery got him carpeted and dismissed from the trainee pilot course.

Apart from all the boxing and storytelling and entertainment at Henlow the main event going on at 13 MU at that time was the assembly of fighter planes arriving from North America. Although I was not trained as an engine mechanic I became part of the team preparing the Merlin engines for these planes. I was part of the team adding the ancillary parts such as generators, fuel pumps, filters and the many other bits and pieces - which I now have a job remembering - but I do remember that I enjoyed it. In the latter part of my time at the MU the work changed to carrying out modifications to Wellington bombers which had been brought back from the Middle East for that purpose.

Every Saturday at around midday there was always an exodus from the camp. God knows what would have happened if the Germans had attacked on Saturday afternoon. It probably kept some people awake at night. Maybe all the Germans also went home for the weekend, although I doubt it. Anyway, it doesn't bear thinking about. At Henlow most airman and women went off by train to London which took only about an hour.

Not everyone used the train. Some went to other destinations by bus, and there were also the hitchhikers. One of these was another PTI who was a wrestler of some repute, and who always took up his position on the road outside the camp to hitch a ride. A car would inevitably pull up and he would get in with his little case, but once, as they drove along, the driver got chatty and grinned and wondered aloud if the PTI might have some little titbits in the case from the cookhouse. "Oh, yes," nodded the bold

PTI, "I'm well in with the guys in the cookhouse". It was a great surprise to the PTI to find out that the chap who gave him a lift was in fact an MP – a military policeman in plain clothes who then turned the car around and took the unlucky PTI back to the camp. He was charged and we were all summoned to witness the old fashioned military ceremony where he was stripped of his sergeant's stripes on the parade ground in front of everybody assembled. It was quite an historic thing to behold. We felt sorry for the fellow but it reminded everyone that a war is a war. Historically nothing changes about winning and losing and perhaps you have to give your side an edge even if you have to resort to the moral high ground of an antiquated ceremony.

I had made many new friends as I went along, but one in particular who I had met at Duxford was Wally Charles from Islington in the East End of London, who, like me, would become a Flight Engineer. When Wally and I ran into each other again at Henlow he began to invite me to visit his home for the weekend. His mother was into her third marriage to someone I was introduced to as Mr Bone, so I called her Mrs Bone. They could never do enough to make me feel at home and I got to see quite a bit of London.

Mrs Bone was a fine woman and on Sundays on my visits she would get all the food for the traditional midday meal prepared early and then, as midday approached, it would all be put on the stove while we went off the local pub while it cooked. The preparation and timing were almost an art and this was what a lot of people in London did on a Sunday. I've never really been one for visiting pubs to drink lots of beer but I'm far from a killjoy and always loved going out with Wally's family on these occasions. They were a joy to be with. Mr Bone seemed quite an elderly gentleman to me but he probably wasn't that old at all and we got on very well. When he found out that I had done a little boxing he told me that he had been a bare fist fighter in his younger days. He told me that his training for fights consisted of skipping to Scottish dance music and steeping his hands in brine. He had a great sense of humour and sometimes as the two of us passed each other we would square up for a little mock-fight fun and we'd feint and bob and weave.

On a visit to Petticoat Lane market where most of East London seemed to be "of a Sunday morning", there was a young man doing a strongman act with chest expanders and challenging anybody to pull them out. "Roll up, roll up" shouted his barker and I just couldn't resist it. I had used expanders for some time before joining up and had become quite adept, so I took up the challenge and he handed them over for me to have a go. To his consternation, I raised my arms above my head, and pulled them right out. Now, this was not the normal way that expanders are pulled out, it's hard, but I could do it. Anyway it was all good fun and the look on his face as I did it and received a spontaneous round of applause from the other punters is still with me to this day. It was all amateur showmanship and definitely a bit of showing off but, like I say: I have never been able to resist a challenge. If somebody asks me to do something or join in, or join up, I have always done it. I'm there. From the LDV to the boxing team, just give me the pen.

Those Sundays in the East End were great fun but after leaving Henlow I never saw Wally again. He became the Flight Engineer that he wanted to be but he met his end on a mission over Germany. The official story was that his plane was shot down and he bailed out and died in the fall. Perhaps he bailed out and was killed by civilians. That sort of thing was common in those terrible times and I don't really know, but I still can't help thinking about the difference between Farmer McLean's treatment of Rudolf Hess in a Scottish field with his pitchfork at the ready, and the treatment that was perhaps meted out to Wally. I saw out the winter of 1943/44 at Henlow and around the end of March 1944 I received notice to begin the course to become a Flight Engineer.

Lord's Cricket Ground - 1944

I had to make my way into London to St. John's Wood where the RAF Reception Centre was situated and where, for the next few weeks, like all the other potential aircrew, I would be given accommodation in local buildings that had been requisitioned, and medically examined and sounded out. Our gathering place for parades was Lord's Cricket Ground. Perhaps I should have written to the newspaper in Strathaven and got them to announce that Bill Leggate of the RAF had finally made it from the fledgling local cricket club to the top table, but that's not really my style.

This was the ground where, before the war, the finest players in the world had walked out to the middle with their bat. Men like England's Len Hutton and the Aussie Don Bradman. I wasn't the only one with those kinds of thoughts in mind. There was quite a batch of us from all over the world at Lord's and as we looked around there was a general air of respect at our surroundings. Many of us had been in the same places and old friendships were renewed and yarns began flowing. I met up with an airman from my own home town called Leslie Bain who was very much liked back home. He was a bit of a card.

One of the first things I said to Leslie was that we should be going home on leave sometime soon and if he went first and spoke to my parents, or anyone else for that matter, he was not to divulge the fact that my new training course had anything to do with flying in a real aeroplane, because if my mum and dad found out they would worry themselves sick. However, it was all to no avail. Leslie got some leave before me and although my words had probably gone in, he got tanked up one night and told some friends about meeting me in London and where it was all headed. That Bill Leggate was training to be a Flight Engineer. Of course, word went around town and in next to no time my parents had found out. I never saw Leslie again but I met his brother after the war. He told me that Leslie had stayed on in the RAF and been killed in a plane crash in 1950 in Aden.

From Pony Boy to Paradise Beach 53

Life is strange. In the evenings at St. John's Wood we could go into the West End of London to go to the dances or the cinema. I like dancing and the place I went most while I was there was Covent Garden Opera House, which had been turned into a dance hall for the duration. I liked it a lot. In the centre of the hall was the platform for the dance bands which was turned back to front as one band took a break and a new one played. It was quite a place. Even now if family are gathered, or I'm somewhere and there's dancing going on, I often tell people I was once a dancer at Covent Garden in London *"don't you know?"*

During WW2 Lord's Cricket Ground was officially occupied by the RAF and on Saturday July 29th 1944, during a very serious match between the RAF and the Army, the players and the 3000 spectators all looked up as they heard the fateful sound of the engine of a V-1 flying bomb cutting out overhead. This meant that the doodlebug, as they were called, which was like a rocket, would drop down and cause the usual carnage. The match had started late due to rain but right then it was in full swing with Jack Robertson of the Army batting. Everybody cursed, threw themselves to the ground and just waited for the inevitable. As it turned out, the bomb landed nearby, but when play resumed, to show absolute defiance and what he thought of the Germans and their flying bombs, Jack Robertson hit the next ball for a towering six – the equivalent of a home run in baseball. He got a standing ovation from *both* sides.

N.B. It's said that in 1934 a delegation from the Boy Scouts travelled to Germany to try and interest the Hitler Youth in the game, and to see whether they might sign up and play matches against cricketing countries around the world. It's also said that, while there was a certain amount of interest from the German authorities, some of our chaps expressed doubts about the German's sense of fair play.

By the time the inevitable happened and we had to leave for new postings, new friendships had begun and new tales and old tales had been told and retold, but there's a tale worth telling here. It's about an easy-going young Irishman called Paddy Burns - and as there are some "Burns" in my wife's family tree, they may well be related. Anyway, the telling of the story itself had in fact begun on parade at the cricket ground. Paddy was ordered to *"Git your hair cut"!* All sergeants loved to bellow that command. The story illustrates how it's always a small world and that life goes on after war and carries over into new times and contemporary days.

A young man called Norman Smith, later known as "Hurricane" Smith, was desperate to join the RAF after he had looked up into the sky from his family back yard in Tottenham and shaken his fist at a flight of German bombers overhead. During the war he flew gliders out of Tarrant Rushton airbase in Dorset but he had once received the same *"Git your hair cut!"* order when summoned to the RAF in St. John's Wood and sent on parade at Lord's Cricket Ground. Before I tell you what happened to Smith *after* WW2 let's go back to Paddy Burns who had shouted *"Yes, Sir!"* to his haircut order.

Now, Paddy, who had a lovely head of wavy hair which was clearly way too long for the NCO's liking, gave us all his usual big Irish smile but made no moan or comment. However, when we saw him again, his nice new short back and sides haircut had revealed a big scar on the back of his head that had been hidden before. Of course we all wanted to know how he got it: *"How did you get that scar, Paddy?"* At first he was reluctant to tell us anything but with a little persuasion he opened up with quite a tale. It seems that he had been a corporal mechanic on a Catalina seaplane based in Murmansk. The purpose of the Catalina was to search that area for signs of German fleet movements, because our convoys carrying supplies to Russia had to pass through those icy waters and they always suffered great losses on the way. My elder brother John, who was in the Royal Navy, endured great hardship while on convoy duty in the extreme winter weather up in that region. Paddy continued with his tale and told us that after doing their stint in Murmansk the crew were withdrawn to the UK, and after a bit of leave they were sent to Gibraltar where they flew out over the Bay of Biscay in search of German U-boats - until one day when they were shot down off the Spanish coast.

The crew all made it ashore, mostly in one piece with nothing life-threatening, but Paddy had got quite a nasty whack and was bleeding badly. After attending to him as best they could, they rested up for a few hours before deciding to set off for Gibraltar on foot. It was a hazardous journey. They had to duck and dive to stay clear of the police – or anyone for that matter. Paddy said that they never really expected to make it but in fact they did against all the odds. It was not only a long journey but a hard one. They could trust nobody. In WW2 Spain was technically a neutral country, but everyone knew they supported the Axis. They arrested anyone without papers and threw them in jail. After many days Paddy and his crew managed to reach Gibraltar and sneak across the border. Paddy's wound had more or less healed itself but without proper stitches had left the big scar. Later the crew were all sent home to the UK.

And that's why Paddy always tried to keep his hair on the long side - to hide the scar. Otherwise people like us would be forever asking how he got it, and he would be constantly telling the tale. When he had finished he gave us all that big smile of his and admitted that he made one exception and that was with the ladies. They loved the romance and the whole daring-do of the story and if he was sorely in need of a good chat-up line, he told them the story and they fell in love with him. After that, every time I saw a Catalina I thought of Paddy and his mates legging it through Spain in the twilight. Interestingly, in 1942, around the time that Paddy was flying off Spain, a Catalina was used in a top secret disinformation plot designed to fool the enemy about the plans and the date of the Allied invasion of Italy. In the real life double bluff a 'drowned' courier was washed onto a Spanish beach with secret documents. German spies swallowed the scam, hook line and sinker, and many lives were saved when the invasion took place. The story was shown in the film, The Man Who Never Was.

Now let me tell you about Norman Smith who had to lie about his age ("the war got in the way") to join EMI as an apprentice recording engineer in their studios (in St. John's Wood). At first, and rather like me being pony boy at Dungavel, and clearing up the dog mess, they had given Norman, the ex-RAF glider pilot, a broom to sweep up the place. He worked hard and worked his way up to be in charge of the Beatles audition and to record 14 of their number one hits. Then he signed and produced another very successful band called *Pink Floyd*. One day in the studio canteen in 1968 he had told the long-haired band members the story about an order he was once given on parade just up the road at Lord's. Far from being miffed the band understood immediately and persuaded Norman to shout "*Git your 'air cut*" on one of their new recordings to mimic that very same parade ground order. It's there, it's on one of the band's recordings called *Corporal Clegg*, and it's from their album *A Saucerful of Secrets*.

One last coincidence with Norman Smith is that he was born in 1922 – the same year as the girl that I was destined to marry - and grew up in the same neighbourhood as her and her father Steve. He was a Spurs football club fan and in the sixties he produced a long-playing record with all the members of the Spurs team of that time singing songs including the Spurs anthem Glory, Glory, Tottenham Hotspurs.

RAF St. Athan – where I met my wife

It was fate. Fate dealt me the most wonderful hand. Fate sent me to St. Athan in South Wales. Then Fate set my lady down on the dance floor of a village hall.

After a week of being sorted out at the cricket ground we were split up and sent on various courses at different locations throughout the UK. Our particular group was sent to South Wales and the largest RAF establishment in the country which was called St. Athan. There, we were to do the actual Flight Engineer course over a period of about four months. St. Athan also guarded the major industrial ports of Cardiff, Swansea and Bristol, as well as the vast coal mines in the Vale of Glamorgan. Coal kept the Fleet at sea and kept the trains running. Without it we would have been lost. The facilities at St. Athan were good, with a camp cinema and a proper swimming pool. It was also handy for transport to many places including Cardiff. However, as we had arrived at the camp about two weeks before the course was due to start we were all given purposeful jobs around the camp to keep us out of mischief – jobs like helping out in one of the dining halls, serving meals and sweeping up and keeping the place tidy.

At an earlier introduction to the flight engineer course we had all been given the choice regarding which type of aircraft we would like to be trained on. There was quite a choice: Lancasters, Halifaxes, Catalinas and Liberators. Generally they were all four engine jobs except for the Catalina. I had decided that my choice would be the Liberator. I had a love of the sea and the Liberator was a great Coastal Command plane so it had to be my first choice. When the course started we were moved to a different part of the camp where the classrooms were located and then we began the basics of the course. I made a good number of new friends and as usual there were a few characters among them who kept our billet a good source of fun and entertainment.

It was at this time, about three weeks into the course, when some of my new mates opted to visit the local village church hall where at times the minister put on dances for the service men and women and for the local community as well. The ticket money was put towards the benefits of the airbase. About six or seven of us went to the event and a good time was had by all. That night was a very special one for me because I danced with a pretty airwoman who took my fancy. Now, back in those far off days there were generally one or two of what were called "excuse me" dances where the young men could tap any other male dancer on the shoulder and then dance off with the girl. The theory and chivalry didn't always work. How could it when it depended completely on the good nature of everyone concerned? I was being tapped on the shoulder a little too often. However, God was smiling down on me and my mates who were standing and watching and had realised what was happening so, every time I lost my partner, one of them would soon step forward and take her away from the interloper and just dance her around to where I was standing and pass her back to me. It could have caused a punch up – and I had seen that happen before - but that night it didn't. As I said, God was smiling down at me and Fate stayed true instead of fickle.

That night I had the pleasure of escorting Marjorie back to her billet, and for the rest of the course we went out in the evenings and at weekends. We also went walking in the countryside around St. Athan and Formby and went dancing in local villages. We went wherever there was a dance advertised - to places like the resort of Barry Island, just making the most of our time together. We compared notes about our background and families. I was a bred in the bone Scot, and Marjorie - who I had soon started calling Madge and she didn't mind - was from London. With the war on and never knowing where we might be from one week to the next, romantically inclined people tended to reveal their personal stories at a faster pace than might otherwise have been the case.

Marjorie's life had begun in the loving home of Steve and Sophie Knight in Tottenham, North London. Her dad was an invalid from World War One where he had served in France. He had also been involved in the disaster that was the ill-fated invasion of the Dardanelles in Turkey, where casualties rivalled that of the Western Front. In one place or another Steve had been wounded, gassed, and contracted malaria. Despite all this he was not full of self-pity and remained cheerful and optimistic and faced up to the problems in his early married life.

There had been a shortage of work and Steve had taken anything he could get. Meanwhile, Sophie, who had trained as a French polisher with a company called Lebus of London, was the main provider. However, there were also other family members who lived close by and they all got on well and so helped each other out. This was obviously a great blessing. The house at Tottenham Hale was their first family home but, in 1935, when Marjorie was thirteen, the Knight family had taken on one of the new properties being built at a place called Enfield Wash. This was where Marjorie lived with her mum and dad until joining the WAAFs and meeting me. Our backgrounds were very different but no deterrent to the way we felt about each other and a little before I left St. Athan we got engaged.

Even so, at that time it would have been beyond my wildest imaginings in that small Welsh village in 1944 to think that Marjorie and I would go on to achieve sixty eight years of marriage and produce five sons. One evening early in June 1944, she and I had arranged to go dancing at a place called Bindals, which sat on the edge of the Bristol Channel, near to Barry Port. We arrived a little early for the dancing, so we went for a stroll on that lovely summer's evening and sat down on a high point looking out over the Bristol Channel. We were so much in love and so immersed in our own little world that it took us some time before we realised that something big was going on down in the Channel below.

From our vantage point we saw the decks of dozens of ships of all types and sizes passing by under our astonished gaze. A huge flotilla was quietly making its way down the coast and slipping out to sea. A few days later, when the news finally spread, we found out that we had been watching part of the Allied invasion fleet on the move as they headed for the D-day landings on the Normandy coast. It was awe-inspiring to think that we were all a part of such a huge scheme as Operation Overlord, and that the beginning of the end was on the way - although we weren't fully aware of it then.

By then we had been in the war for a long time and sometimes it seemed that it might never end. For our generation the war had become a way of life and we just got on with it. I loved working on the Liberator aircraft.

Practically everything on board was worked by electricity including the gun turrets. The only weak point of the Lib was the fact that, if it did have to ditch in the sea, the crew would only have one minute to abandon it and get out due to the strange design of the bomb doors, which collapsed inwards. Their construction was in the style of a venetian blind, and in the later part of our Liberator training our rehearsals for making a very orderly but a very swift exit were a priority.

Our course at St. Athan came to a close. All of us passed and were given postings to our next phase of training. Incredibly, I was being sent to Nassau in the Bahamas for operational training. Me! Sent to Nassau! It was like something out of an adventure novel: the Caribbean Sea, pirates and palm trees. Looking back, I couldn't really take it in, and I *didn't* really take it in at the time because wherever I was posted meant that Marjorie and I had to part and to say goodbye for a while. We could only hope to see each other in the near future and none of us was sure what the future would hold. Nothing was certain. Hope was about all we had to hold onto and there was a lot of that about.

Arriving somewhere and leaving had now become a way of life for me and for many of us with all the postings over the years, and to a certain extent I was always mentally primed to go. It was always off to new places, new friends, new trainings and experiences. This time I felt a little bit low. Many of my new mates had opted for the heavy bombers. It was August 1944 and nobody really had a clue how long the war would go on. We were supposed to be winning now and were beginning to bomb Germany into submission but it was still against intense resistance. Not everyone would survive, and of course the Germans had some new rockets and there was the constant rumour of other secret weapons.

Before I could be trained for ops on the palm tree-flanked beaches of Nassau, it was decided that I should attend Air Gunnery School at Pembrey Sands which was also in South Wales. It was a two month course. The school was hidden amongst marshland and sand dunes, behind miles of concealing forest that ran alongside the Bristol Channel quite near to the town of Llanelli. There was a sandy beach close to the airfield and on good days we made our way there for a swim in the Channel after training, but to go for a swim we had to be careful and follow a designated path through a minefield. *My God! Through a minefield to take a dip in the sea!* Would any part of our life ever be the same again?

Early in the war the airfield had been home to Spitfires. Later Hurricanes had arrived with members of the Polish Air Force and they became known as *The City of Warsaw Hurricane Squadron.* Their job was to protect the Royal Ordnance Factory that was tucked away in the dunes at Pembrey Burrows. The factory was the largest producer of TNT in the country, and was one of the first places to be bombed by the Luftwaffe early in the war. A nearby foundry not only produced bomb casings but also steel parts for the mobile Mulberry Harbours that were used in the D-Day Normandy Landings. Guarding all these plants and places was vital and planes from Pembrey could be scrambled and airborne fast. Eventually, the Poles departed and were replaced by other squadrons. American troops had also arrived and had trained there on six-wheeled amphibious vehicles known as DUKW's - affectionately known as Ducks - before departing to board ships at Swansea Docks. There had been constant change, constant alertness and vigilance.

The USA, Canada and The Bahamas - 1944

Most of the Americans that had been around the area had left on that huge flotilla that Madge and I had observed that evening a few weeks earlier from the cliffs above the Bristol Channel, with the Mulberries and Ducks being towed to the rear of the big war ships and troop carriers, all heading for D-day.

Now, strange things tend to happen when the opposition is put on the back foot. Some people take stock of their own side's chances and decide to make a deal. One such event took place at Pembrey when a German fighter plane came over the airfield and then, as men raced to their action stations and prepared to blast him and any others that were with him out of the sky, he came in to land.

Perhaps the German was an educated man and had read that in 540 A.D. an Irish monk called Tathan had been blown off course across the Irish Channel and ran aground in Wales where he convinced the locals about his plight and they took him in and he was able to found his own monastery – which he called St. Athan. However, this was Pembrey Sands not St. Athan and, whatever the German flyer's excuse was going to be, the air controller on duty was taking no chances. He was quick to react and I think he sized up the situation very well. As the enemy plane landed and taxied towards the control tower, he was up and out with the first weapon he could find which happened to be his Verey pistol which he fired occasionally when one of our planes was coming in to land and the pilot hadn't noticed that his wheels had not come down yet. He armed the flare gun and pointed it straight ahead as he made his way towards the plane. When the pilot opened the canopy the controller pointed the flare gun at him and ordered him to put his hands up shouting *"Hande hoch!"*

The German pilot didn't seem at all fazed. "I'm lost," he shouted in German. He later insisted that he had genuinely thought our airfield was a German airfield. After he was carted off and questioned he said that when he was crossing (what he now understood to be) the Bristol Channel, he thought he was crossing the English Channel on his way to Occupied France. Exactly where he was flying from in the first place in order to get all these things wrong or backwards in one fell swoop, he didn't elaborate on. However, bizarre flying and lousy navigating aside, his plane was one of the latest Messerschmitt 109's, so most people reckoned he was a straight defector, and, if he *was* defecting, then a brand new ME 109 was a very nice present to have brought with him.

By the time I started at the gunnery school, the D-day invasion had happened and the action had moved on inland to the battlefields of France, Belgium and Holland. It was onwards through Europe as fast as possible with generals like our own Montgomery (Monty), and the Americans like Bradley and Patton. We did various types of gun training from simulators, and even worked with shotguns doing skeet shooting. We did air to sea and air to air. We fired from the turret of an Avro Anson at a "drogue" which was pulled through the sky by a Miles Master and the ammunition we fired was tipped with paint. Each novice gunner had bullets of a different colour so that when the drogue was examined after the exercise it was easy to count how many hits were made, and by whom, by simply checking the colours.

One day an incident occurred that could have been tragic. It also reminded everyone that even though the war was approaching its end, if you didn't watch out you could still become a casualty, a statistic. Well, on this particular day a trainee was firing and, while making his allowance for the tow-plane's speed as he aimed at the drogue, he was far too generous and his bullets raked the plane. The pilot was a lucky man and when he landed he ignored everybody, kept on walking and headed for the nearest pub. "You need a bit of luck", said our course instructor. Then he told us that he himself had once been shot down over France and had luckily been rescued by the French Underground. They had helped him in eluding the Nazis and getting back to the UK in one piece. "Yes," he mused as he nodded his head, "you do need a bit of luck. Just don't rely on it, that's all."

Good advice, and with my gunnery course completed, Madge and I got lucky and were able to take a spot of leave together. We made our way up to Strathaven to spend some time together and for her to meet all of my family – all her future in-laws. After our shared leave, Madge went back to her base and I made my familiar way by train to Blackpool to be checked out and examined yet again and to get prepared for my journey to Nassau in the West Indies. There I would begin operational training on the Liberators with Coastal Command.

"So, you're off on holiday, are you?"

In terms of cold-hearted statistics, at one stage of the war the production of warplanes began to outstrip the production of aircrews. Aircrews were, tragically, being lost very fast. So the idea was to train some of the new crews somewhere so far out of the way that the Luftwaffe couldn't bother them. Planes, especially the Liberators, were ferried to Nassau OTU (operational training unit) where crews were trained on them. They also staffed Coastal Command out of Nassau. Some Libs were ferried across the Atlantic to enter service in Europe. The Lib also had long-range capabilities so it was a good plane for the Far East.

However, at the camp in Blackpool, being posted to Nassau was still seen as a "cushy number" by the briefing officers. It was desirable and exotic and therefore the duty of those officers to give the guys who were being posted to Nassau a hard time, and to treat them with the appropriate amount of scorn – "So, you're off on holiday, are you?"

From Blackpool it was back by train to Scotland and to Greenock where we were to join our ship at a place called the Tail of the Bank, a safe anchorage for ocean-going ships. Ours was a large modern Dutch vessel called the Nieuw (New) Amsterdam which had been built in Holland and weighed about 40,000 tons. The New Amsterdam had been a luxury ocean-going liner before the war had begun and was known as the "Darling of the Dutch". It was 750 feet long which, if you want a rough guide, is exactly two and a half football pitches in length. So it was big and at the time it was the fifth largest passenger liner in the world.

Launched just as WW2 broke out, its first job was to take the Dutch royal family off to a safe exile for the duration and then it was turned over to the Allies for the war effort, eventually making forty-four trips across the Atlantic, dodging U-boats. It had been transformed from a luxury liner to a troopship in no time at all. Gone were the fine dining rooms and all the ornate bars with the expensive liquor and the music and chandeliers. Gone were all luxuries along with thousands of deck chairs. She had been

From Pony Boy to Paradise Beach

refitted with the bare essentials. The New *Amsterdam* wartime troopship had been put together with one thing in mind which was this: how many servicemen could be crammed on board and fed and then, hopefully, delivered alive onto dry land before these men headed off to the battlefields or back home.

On our voyage to New York there were ten thousand passengers, including two thousand prisoners of war and also many Americans who had been wounded. Our deck was set up with hammocks and I presumed it was likewise on the other decks that I never saw.

The following piece - which I hope will illustrate what it was like on board - was written from memory by a US soldier called Galbraith who travelled on the ship. Part of what he wrote has been reprinted here with the kind permission of his son Bob, and I have added some of my own memories about the trip. The photo showing how men were accommodated is from the archives of the US Navy.

"I was one of approximately five hundred men packed into a room located at the bow of the New Amsterdam. Our room used to be the ship's cinema. When my buddy Joe Bernal commented that we were packed in like sardines, someone else agreed and added that there was everything but the oil. There were steel stanchion pipes extending from the floor to the roof. Bunks were attached to these pipes and stacked about eight high in some areas. The bunks were about two feet wide by six feet long. They each had a pipe frame and inside that frame a rectangular piece of strong canvas which was stretched tightly above the bunk and strung through metal eyelets on the edge of the canvas, and by wrapping the strong cord around the pipe frame. This gave a little bit of give to these bunks. The bunks themselves touched head to toe.

On one side of your bunk was a two foot wide aisle. If you were up high you had to climb up to your bunk using other guy's bed frames in your stack as a ladder and then try to get yourself horizontal before sliding sideways into your bunk. Sometimes when a crowd of us came back from chow at the same time we were like a colony of monkeys swinging through the trees and grabbing for anything to hold on to. You had to be very careful where you trod because, with tempers constantly at a flashpoint - often from losing money in dice games and poker games in the toilets –

one clumsy step could cause a fight that would escalate into a drunken saloon on a Saturday night type of mass brawl.

Added to this, you had to stow all your gear in the bunk with you, and that included a steel helmet, a gas mask, a backpack, duffel bag, overcoat, and blankets. Some men also kept their rifles in their bunk, while others hung them from the pipe frame making for another obstacle. So how did it all get stashed away and still leave space for a man? Well, it didn't and to sum it all up (in two words as movie mogul Sam Goldwyn once said) it was "im-possible."

However, somehow it got done, but the worst thing of all - and that includes the tension and the fear and the stench and the lack of air and the sickness and your aching bones - was the fact that the catering was done by the Brits; or it was done under the supervision of British cooks. It didn't matter. It was terrible. Cooks? These guys didn't cook, they mangled and murdered and the menu may as well have been an obit" `

Galbraith

The Americans hated the food with a passion but – and I can't explain this - I remembered the food rather differently. There was a rota of cooks and there were five sittings with colour coded cards. Maybe we got lucky and we got locked into a competent cook shift? Or maybe there were different kitchens on different decks. After all, the ship was catering for 10,000. I do remember writing to Madge and telling her that on the six day crossing we got two good meals per day, but that what I loved most was the beautiful little loaves which were baked on board and were a part of our meals during the journey.

A few years ago a friend of mine told me he once took his father (an army man who served in the East Kents in WW2), and his mother (who had been in the WAAF's) to the USA on holiday, and they all went to an army-themed restaurant where there was a perimeter fence around the building. The music was continual Glenn Miller, and they served individual little loaves with meals. He said he honestly didn't think he would ever get them to leave the place.

I also wrote to Madge and told her our meals were served by German POW's who were specially selected for the journey. Some of them readily admitted to us that at one time they had been staunch Nazis but, since they had been captured, and since they were now on a ship being hunted by U-boats in wolf packs, they had come to see Herr Hitler in another light.

We tried to get on deck for some air as often as possible and to watch the flying fish that leapt and flew alongside the ship. Unfortunately, on the deck directly above us was a specified German Area, where they used to exercise some of the German prisoners who hadn't yet "seen the light", and you had to watch out because some of them got seasick. Overall, I enjoyed the new experience of being on board a big ship. There was some tension because U-boats were very active in the North Atlantic. It was a bit like being on an airfield expecting a raid and we knew we followed an individual and secret route laid down by the Admiralty and known only to the captain and senior crew, who opened up their orders only *after* we set off.

The highlight of the whole - and for many quite nerve-racking - trip came as we approached New York at about seven in the morning and just about everyone who could make it on deck went out to view the Manhattan skyline. Many of the Americans were being repatriated from the battlefields and they were visibly moved. To them, as to us, New York was a sight to behold. Fifty years later, almost to the day, I enjoyed the same view from the Queen Elizabeth 2 liner, but the second time I was with Madge, on a trip to celebrate our golden wedding anniversary.

But then, back in WW2, we disembarked and immediately boarded a train which would take us in the exact opposite direction to the Bahamas. We joked that *"the army must be in charge, then"*. We were informed that we were going to the Caribbean via Montreal in Canada, via a place called Lachine Airfield. Once we were on the train we forgot all about the route and a four-hundred mile trip as a team of American ladies came along passing out doughnuts and drinks. It was a lovely welcome to the USA and it got even better when we finally arrived at Lachine Camp where there was a spread of food laid out for us that took our breath away. After years of wartime rationing in Britain it was like a banquet and very few of us had ever seen the like.

A Hitch-hiker's Guide to Hospitality and Strange Adventures in 1944
Part 1: Hospitality

We had fourteen days leave before the course got started down in Nassau, so we spent a few days getting acquainted with Montreal and then I teamed up with a couple of the lads to go back down to New York City and have a proper look. When we had first arrived we had been piled onto a train fast, and never got a chance to do any sightseeing, so we got to thinking about being in New York. It was like something out of the movies. We thought we should go and have a little adventure.

The names of my two mates were Arthur Wood and Sam Wood and they were not related. There was some paperwork to complete because we would be going back over the US/Canadian border but once that was done we set off hitchhiking south and, being innocents abroad, soon discovered we were on the wrong road. I was reminded about the German pilot with the brand new ME 109 who flew over the wrong sea to the wrong airfield in the wrong country – or so he told the controller with the flare pistol - and so I told the lads the story while we waited for a ride.

We soon got back on the right track. Hitchhiking was very easy when you were in uniform, and we made good time, but we didn't get all the way to New York because our final lift only went as far as Albany, which is the capital of New York State. So we decided that it was a very nice place for a spot of leave. Our visit also turned out to be unusual. When the three of us arrived in the early morning and with people all around us on their way to work, our first priority had been to find somewhere to stay and get off the street. Where better than the YMCA? So we found a hostel on one of the main streets, went in, booked accommodation, and after getting our bags locked safely away we were back on the busy street.

While we were standing out there on the sidewalk in front of the hostel and wondering what to do first, or next, and just like in any move-it-along film script, a very smartly dressed lady came up to us and said: "OK. Where are you boys staying?" Of course, we all pointed behind us at the same time at the YMCA and said, "Right here". That's when she shook her head firmly and said that for the duration of our visit we would be staying at her place. OK. Yes, ma'am. All three of us were now getting the hang of the lingo as she ordered us back in to check out and collect our gear. She was taking us home. So we got our bags back from the bemused hostel clerk and went trailing off behind her.

Arriving at her place she showed us our room, gave us a front door key and then went off to work at a store where she was apparently head of the fur department. It was a wonderful display of American hospitality and trust and typical of all that the airmen could expect on that break from discipline. Wherever they went in Canada or America, people were open and friendly and determined to take us under their wings. I'll never forget her. The lady's name was Mrs Barton, and while she worked in the fur department of a big department store, her husband, Mr Jim Barton, was head of the largest fingerprint department in America – which just happened to be in Albany. In fact, even now, Albany seems to be the home of the "fingerprinting biz" and even has a company called Fingerprint America which sells 5 million home printing kits a year. Back in 1944, while we were there, he invited us to visit his place of work and showed us around. He showed us the large fingerprint machine which – as we watched - was going about its work of picking out the criminals and – for elimination purposes - discarding the dabs of the good guys. Then he also took us to the photographic department and showed us some pictures of 'real-life' corpses and mutilated bodies from cases that were being investigated at that time. It was shocking, it was gruesome, it was fascinating and it was a real insight into early criminal forensics; the kind of thing you read about in crime novels or saw in films before the internet and mobile phones and DNA. Few civvies ever got such a personal tour.

The Bartons were a lovely couple and Mrs B also invited us to visit her at the store where she worked. It was huge, and far bigger than we imagined. She took us around and introduced us to just about everybody from the counter staff to the managing director. We were also excused from imposing ourselves too much on Mrs Barton at her home, with regards to her feeding us, because Albany had loads of well stocked canteens for servicemen where you could get a cheap meal at practically any time of day. You could also pick up free tickets to theatres and various events happening in town.

Although our visit didn't coincide with Thanksgiving which is a really big family celebration in the USA in late November, some of the Barton's relatives, a niece and her husband, were down from Montreal on a visit and Mrs Barton decided to cook us all a proper Thanksgiving meal. She cooked a turkey and all the trimmings and she made a fine job of it, too. The niece and her husband invited us to stay with them when we returned to Canada, which we did and they made us very welcome indeed.

Part 2: Strange Adventures

Our stay in Albany flew by and one morning we said goodbye to our hosts and started on our way back north. We were soon out on the main highway hoping for a quick lift, but this part of our trip turned out to be more than just a leisurely ride back to Montreal. An adventure began with the first car we thumbed which was a big black saloon with just a driver on board. It pulled up and the guy enquired where we were going. When we said Montreal he said he'd take us there but as soon as we were underway he asked if any of us drove. One of my mates, Sam or Arthur, I can't remember which, said he did, and the driver said he was going to stop and leave us and then return with another car to continue on our journey.

All very strange, certainly, but we went along with it. After all, what did we have to lose? We were three tough guys in the RAF so what did we have to fear? He soon returned with another big black saloon and decided that Woody, my driver-mate and I would travel in this second car, while Woody my other mate would travel with him in the lead. This was still all very strange and slightly disconcerting but we set off at a fair lick. It was now the middle of September and the trees were at their best with all the leaves in full glory - *War? What war?*

The scenery alone made the drive worthwhile, although, now, as I run the reels of our American Adventure in my head, I remember that I was half expecting the lead car to stop at a bank any moment and our new friend to pull out a Tommy gun, pull his hat down lower and excuse himself for a few minutes to do some business, saying: *"Keep the motor ticking over."* It occurred to me, as I sat and let my mind wander, that sometime soon we might become clients of Mr Barton and his fingerprint department after we hit the bank, ditched the cars, stole a couple of new ones, and headed for the hills with a bagful of cash.

However, after a while the lead car pulled into a diner and we followed. Our host treated all of us. He was obviously up to something but nobody asked him what it was and soon we were off again at the same crazy speed as before until we arrived at the gates of a big house. What would happen here? Well, here, we'd just say thanks and goodbye, leaving both cars. We were back on our own, walking along the highway and keeping our eye out for another ride. We didn't have to wait long. This time it was an old banger with just a driver. We crammed ourselves in and were soon chatting happily away.

But, as I've said before, things are hardly ever what they seem to be at first glance. It wasn't long before our new driver sighed and told us unhappily that he was returning from the railway station. He said he had just split up with his wife and had put her on a train back to her parents. He drove along muttering about his problems until we arrived at a place called Burlington where he said his own parents lived. Again, we were shown wonderful hospitality. They insisted on inviting us in for a meal and then asked us to stay for a few days to see some of the town. We agreed and they made us very comfortable at their home which was joined onto a small garage and petrol station from which they obviously made their living.

After the evening meal on our second day our hosts suggested that their son take us into town to see a movie. So off we went the four of us but – and here we go again - outside the cinema the son said he had some important business to attend to. We should go on into the movie by ourselves, he said. He would meet us after it finished; and he did. We were getting the hang of America, by then. We agreed that what you did is you stood outside the movie house or the YMCA or wherever you had fetched up, and somebody picked you up and took you somewhere else and gave you dinner and a bed. What a country. Then the son turned up looking rather nervous and said that he'd gone off to see his wife but her father had been waiting for him with a shotgun. He said it was probably just to scare him off.

On the third day in Burlington, after dinner, we were about to say goodbye when, against our protests, the son's father insisted on paying for bus tickets for us to go on to Montreal. We looked at each other. The son looked nervous and so in the old banger we waited to hear his new plan as he drove us towards the bus station. We could see that he had something on his mind. He was obviously working on some sort of alternate arrangement, which was this: If we gave him our bus tickets he could cash them in and then drive us to Montreal, instead.

We agreed. Why not? We then went on a detour to pick up his wife. We had never learned what had gone wrong with them. There had been no talk about it around the meal table. Mom had not taken any of us aside – as mums often do - and poured her heart out. Pop had not told us what a big mistake the marriage had been. So it was obviously very complicated. Maybe Mom and Pop back at the house with the little garage were in on the new plan? Maybe they had talked about it and the son had shrugged and offered the opinion that his wife's father might get out the shotgun again if he turned up again on his own, but not if he turned up mob-handed. Yes. Because that would mean he'd have to reload his shotgun.

Maybe the trunk of the car was now full of guns hidden under our bags? However, when we got out at the in-laws place there was no sign of any over-protective fathers or any shotguns. The wife was waiting. She didn't say much. It was as though they were eloping *after* the marriage, and if that was the case then the extra bus ticket money might come in handy. Unless, of course, they were really a Bonnie and Clyde type of couple going off to stick up a bank. If so, the bus ticket money would just be "small change". Then other concerns took over as we drove away. We began to wonder whether the overcrowded old banger would even reach Canada. Maybe it just *sounded* like an old banger? Maybe old Pop had installed a supercharger in it on the quiet out there in his little garage? Maybe it was a getaway car?

Someone once gave me a bit of homespun philosophy which went something like: "If you buy the ticket, you've got to take the ride". Well, our ride had a definite start and finish because we were limited by the number of days we were allowed out on the loose. On the return part of the trip from Albany to Lachine Camp we had never been given a real clue as to what was really going on. Not from the man with two cars, and not with the hopeful couple and the troubled and unhappy in-laws. We had never pressed them with too many questions. In effect, we were just passing through someone else's anxiety heartbreak like a car in a rain shower. People who are continually anxious are always wiping the same windows but looking out for another rainbow at the same time. Families can be very strange; at once close and then distant. Sometimes you're not on the same

From Pony Boy to Paradise Beach

road. When you ask directions you get no answers. There is often no magic wand. Sometimes you just have to leave the problem behind and start again. As the son set us down at a convenient spot to get the bus on to Lachine Camp and drove away I silently wished him God Speed.

We had met some wonderful, generous people, and some troubled generous people. We had been in and out of a kind of twilight zone. We had gone from dodging U-boats in the Atlantic to an early Thanksgiving dinner – just in case we never got another one, perhaps. They were normal people who worked with fingerprints and furs. They were Americans, well settled now, but their ancestors had been just like the Norwegian folk who came back to Scotland with the commandoes after the raid in the Arctic. We had been in fast cars on long highways with people who had some heavy things on their minds. There had been some adventure and some intrigue and now we were ready for those white sands, blue-water bays and waving palm trees.

On our arrival back at Lachine we had to prepare for the train journey to Miami to catch a boat to Nassau. The train part of the journey would be around two thousand miles which usually took three or four days. However, with so much military transport on the rails we were told that the journey was currently longer and slower. The route would take us through New York, Washington, Jacksonville and then on to Miami. Just out of interest this is the same train and route that James Bond travelled in the book *Live and Let Die*.

Our sleeping and dining was all done on board. We were all comfortable, and very well catered for. At a number of stops along the way we managed to get off and have a look around and stretch our legs. I enjoyed these postcard sized views of America. It was very much different from wartime Britain and some things were unexpected. As we travelled south we came into areas with segregation laws which also had to be observed on trains and buses and toilets and even on the pavements or sidewalks. South of Washington we travelled on a segregated section of the train. There were members of our party who decided to openly disregard the rules and entered the off limits sections. They were caught, there is no other word for it, and severely reprimanded for their behaviour.

On arrival in Miami we were taken to a hotel and told there was a hurricane heading our way. What about our palm trees and blue waters?

Never mind about that! The hurricane season was still on and it ran from June to November. Instead of sailing off to Nassau the next day, we had to stay in Miami until the worst of it was over. In the end the hurricane veered to the north where it wreaked considerable damage but during the alert my mates and I helped the local shopkeepers who had to board up their premises. They had been delighted at the arrival of so much free help and it was good to give something back.

Nassau, Bahamas - 1944

Eventually we set sail for Nassau, which was about one hundred and eighty miles away into the Caribbean Sea and would take no more than about half a day. It was now the end of October and our arrival in Nassau Harbour was accompanied by local kids who swam around the ship. We were told by the ship's crew that the kids were hoping we would throw money so they could scoop the coins which might be thrown their way. We dug into our pockets for any American change we had and while they called out their names we tossed coins which they stored in their mouths as they swam around.

We were transported to our accommodation near one of the two airfields everybody smiling happily now, taking a keen interest in our new surroundings: here was indeed the aquamarine sea, the silky white sands, bright green trees and tall palms. On either side of the dirt roads we travelled there were typical island houses and shops made of painted clapboard and with gingerbread verandas. You could tell that we were all thinking the same thing - we couldn't ask for a better place to be on holiday. We knew we were there to work but we could always hope for some time to relax. One of our airfields was named after a previous governor, Sir Harry Oakes, but other than that, I knew nothing about him. The island of New Providence - another word for fortune, hope or the grace of God - was so named because this was where Columbus had landed and had first set foot in the Americas. There is a monument to him at Government House in Nassau.

We had been given a little background information and I knew that the Duke of Windsor, formerly the strange and troubled Edward VIII, the ex-King of England, resided there as Governor of the Bahamas, along with his wife, the equally strange Duchess who was formerly an American divorcee named Wallis Simpson. That seemed enough of a curious situation for us to be getting on with.

Of course, I never really expected to actually meet the Windsors, and I didn't. The Duchess "interested herself" – that's the only way I can describe it - in a sort of canteen at the back of Government House. Its facilities were plain and the feel was a bit like an old fashioned youth club where you could hang out and play table tennis and get some tea and a bun – a bit like the Sally Army. For some reason she sold photographs of herself and you could choose one and leave it in an envelope with your name on. My memory may be playing tricks on me but, as I recall, the idea was that she would then sign the photo for you and you picked it up at another time. She was involved in various charities and maybe she donated the photo-money. I don't know. So I've got a photo but no signature. However, one of my sons looked up the price of these photos on the internet and the exact same one that I've got is £475 – *with* her signature.

The internet is a fine thing and while my son was looking up the photos we found some snippets and pieces about the ex-royal couple. It seems that Wallis Simpson was convinced she had stomach cancer and had a consultation in the USA in the July of 1944, and then a "successful" operation in the September – a month before we arrived. There was also some information that said the Duke and Duchess were obsessed with "film noir" and spy movies like *Casablanca,* which came out in 1942 starring Humphrey Bogart and Ingrid Bergman. Apparently, the Duke fancied himself as a spy for the allies. Perhaps they were going to turn the "tea and a bun" canteen into a version of "Rick's Bar"? Incredibly, if you watch the movie with its array of dodgy characters, some of whom might switch sides at any moment, and, if perhaps you're also a bit of a fantasist, you can see where he was coming from – and maybe even the Duchess, too. It's said that the Duke actually put forward the idea of doing some kind of undercover work, but the government thought he was a bit of an on-going disaster and, as we were now winning the war, they couldn't risk it. One of the big lines in *Casablanca* comes near the end where the plane is sitting and waiting on the runway – a DC3 as I remember – it's heading for Lisbon, and then, as she has terrible second thoughts, Bogart reminds Bergman that *"We'll always have Paris."*

With their lives seemingly always playing back-to-front, that's exactly what the Windsors did when they went to live in Paris after the war.

It wasn't until we had been on New Providence for a while that we learned about the very strange story of the murder of the man that our airfield was named after. Sir Harry Oakes had been a Canadian multi-millionaire and the richest man in the Bahamas. He had made his vast wealth from gold mines in Canada and then moved to the Caribbean to protect his fortune in a tax haven. On the night of July 7th 1943, he was brutally murdered by being whacked on the head with a spiked club. Afterwards an attempt had been made to burn the body. Naturally, the Bahamas CID was called in but then, and somewhat controversially, the governor, the Duke of Windsor, had taken the case away from the local CID and called in some homicide detectives that he'd met in Miami. Yes, Miami! You can't help thinking about the Duke's state of mind. It all points to an obsession with "noir" and writers like Raymond Chandler who wrote books like *The Big Sleep* and even PG Wodehouse who was duped or blackmailed by the Germans into making some strange radio broadcasts during the war.

N.B. Apparently, in the Duke's haste to close the murder case and reduce the flak from such a high profile scandal that happened "on his watch", the wrong man had been charged. There has always been a lot of controversy over the years about the killing of Sir Harry Oakes and the rumours and scandal never died. The Duke of Windsor did not come out of the episode smelling like roses. One of the daily newspapers did a feature in August 2005 written by an author called William Boyd. The piece was entitled *Trouble in Paradise.*

However, Paradise was no trouble for me. I loved it and in October 1944 we settled in at the airfield and had a couple of days to get acquainted with the staff who would put us through our operational activities. We were introduced to the first aircraft on which we would train which was the Mitchell B25 bomber. This plane would act as a stepping stone to flying in the Liberators which were four engine jobs as compared to the Mitchell's two. I have learned since then that the Mitchells were the aircraft used to bomb Tokyo for the very first time. They managed this by taking off from US aircraft carriers, going over Tokyo and dropping their bombs, and then just kept on flying to China where they landed.

We had only done a few exercises on the Mitchells when there was a disastrous collision between two of them. The planes were carrying most of the instructors and only one person survived. He was Squadron Leader Rusk who I met about a month later. I think there were ten casualties. A sad affair, but the training carried on more or less as usual although some of us semi-trained flight engineers suddenly had to act as a second "Chiefie" until replacements arrived.

Our training at Nassau was confined to Monday to Friday, and according to rumours at the camp the reason was that the Duke of Windsor did not want the place disturbed at weekends. Well, whatever the reason, it meant that we got time we'd hoped for when we'd first arrived to enjoy the sea and the lovely weather - which, in terms of heat, was comparable to a very, *very* good English summer in Blackpool.

My favourite place was called Paradise Beach. It's still basically the same although I can see from new photos on the net that it's a little bit more developed these days than in 1944. However, when describing it, advertising agencies don't even have to search for superlatives. It's still described thus: *Paradise Beach is secluded and on the north-western tip of Paradise Island: one mile of pristine powder-white sand and warm crystal clear waters, as featured in the James Bond movie Thunderball.*

What else can I say? We used to spend a lot of time there and made good use of the offshore diving station that was built by RAF servicemen and secured out where the water was deep enough. Sometimes I used to stand there on the beach and just drink it all in. Then I'd look at my mates Wally Shaw or Jock Faulkner and they'd say nothing, just grin. To be able to go somewhere like that just once in your life is a wonderful thing. It was hard to remind yourself that there was a war going on.

Once our initial familiarization was completed we began the flying part of the training on Liberators. Crews were formed of two pilots, two navigators, two air gunners, and two wireless operators sometimes doubling up as radar ops or air gunners, one wireless operator doubling mechanic, and me as flight engineer doubling air gunner. Our crew got on fine with commissioned officers and non-coms and I never heard the word "Sir" used during the six months we were together. At Coastal Command the First Pilot was like the captain on a ship being called Skipper; a flight sergeant was called Chief Petty Officer.

We had to complete a number of varied exercises to get through the course. These exercises ranged from dropping practice bombs to getting familiar with the powerful point-five machine guns, of which there were ten. Then there was the radar which we mainly practised at night. We also carried a large naval searchlight of one million candlepower under the right hand wing. In use the radar operator would find the target and inform the skipper of the direction and range and then guide him to the target. When the plane was a mile from the target the searchlight was switched on and bomb doors opened ready to drop depth charges.

In any of the armed forces you will always come across characters and persons of note, and I came across a very fine man in Nassau when I became involved in boxing again. Harry Matthews at Nassau was like Harry Charman at Henlow in that both had been pro boxers for a time. Boxing was one of the accepted ways out of poverty in the old days and Harry Matthews had been a European champ. His sister Jessie Mathews was a famous actress. She was a genuine English rags-to-riches treasure who after the war went on to the title role in the BBC's long-running radio show *Mrs Dale's Diary*. Harry and Jessie came from the Matthews family of about sixteen children, of whom ten or eleven survived, and they'd all grown up behind a butcher's shop in Berwick Street Market in London's Soho. They were poor as church mice but Harry was an absolute gent and a great help to the RAF's young boxers.

With Harry's help, in the Bahamas, I began to box again. I was better at it than I was before and I had learnt a few tricks, but at the only big boxing event I took part in at Nassau I came in second again. I didn't disgrace myself, though. I fought a man called Zimmerman who was more mature and savvy than me. The main bout that night out in the Caribbean was a light heavyweight contest between an RAF man and an American Golden Gloves champion from 1939 who was now in the US marines Corps – N.B. The Golden Gloves competition is famous in the USA and even Mohammed Ali was once a champion back when he was still Cassius Clay. That night, it was a return match. The two fighters had fought before with the American taking the honours first time around, so this was of great interest for the town and RAF personnel. Burton was our man and he was very well-prepared this time around, finishing the fight quickly after two hard-hitting rounds.

As we moved on through the course every newly trained ten-man crew was given notice of their next posting and mine was to the Far East. No sooner had I received news of my posting when two other flight engineers with whom I had become friends came to see me and asked a big favour. It seemed they had been friends for a long time but were constantly being posted to different destinations. They had managed to both be in Nassau, but at the end of the course one was now headed for the Far East, like me, and the other being posted back to the UK. There was only one way around the problem. They wanted to ask – on condition that it was subsequently and officially rubber-stamped - if I would agree to a swap and let both of them head to the Far East. I couldn't believe my luck and I was more than happy to agree. This way I would be reunited with Madge. It was a fantastic deal for me. I often think about these two young men and I even have photographs of them. At that time there was still a fearful and bloody struggle going on with Japan and I often wonder if they survived. I count myself a lucky man with their request.

Meanwhile, still in the land of the palm tree, I now had a new crew to train with and what a good bunch they proved to be under the leadership of skipper Lofty Lamont. One particular friend in my crew was Wallace "Wally" Shaw who was also from Scotland. Christmas and New Year came and went and we spent all our spare time swimming and enjoying as much of the sunshine and tropical island life as we could. I mention Wally in particular because, while many wartime friendships don't last when it's all over, Wally would come back into my life.

Our training ended in mid-January 1945 and we retraced our steps to Miami and then up the Eastern seaboard of America, into the bitter cold of the North and then on into Canada and to Moncton, New Brunswick. There we had to wait until a ship was able to pick us up from Halifax for the journey home. In Canada it was deep winter but with new cold weather RAF uniforms we didn't notice. According to the locals the weather wasn't too severe that year. I remember watching the Petitcodiac River (nicknamed the Chocolate River) that ran through Moncton, and I was surprised to see so much broken ice flowing along so early in the season. After all, it was still January, but maybe the river was in a hurry like we all were. We were even persuaded to try a bit of ice-skating - sometimes in people's back gardens, as well as on proper rinks - but you need plenty of practice or you spend a lot of time on your backside.

Looking back on our leaving Halifax, it's a pity that I never got the time to go and see the graveyard where some of the Titanic dead were laid to rest, because, just recently some photographs from 1912 have come to light, taken by a man called 'Westy' Legate. Whether there is a direct Leggate connection, I don't know.

It was recently the 100th anniversary of the sinking of the RMS Titanic by an iceberg on its maiden voyage in 1912. It went down with great loss of life and it's an anniversary because it's considered to be an historic 'event'.

At the time it was launched and then sank - about ten years before I was born - it was the most up-to-date passenger liner that had ever been built.

Recently I saw a piece about a man called 'Westy' Legate. It seems that he had taken some photographs of a burial-at-sea of some of the drowned passengers from the Titanic that had been picked up while he had been serving as 4th Officer with a cable-laying ship operating out of Canada called the C.S. Mackay-Bennett.

The C.S. stands for cable ship and the Mackay-Bennett, which was built in Glasgow, of course, had been sent to the spot where the Titanic had gone down by the owners of the Titanic. The White Star Line had asked this big favour and the Mackay-Bennett's hardy crew of 75 responded. They loaded up their ship with an embalmer called John Snow, and coffins and body bags, and also the Reverent K.C. Hind from Halifax Cathedral. Then with 100 tons of ice they went out and retrieved 306 of the bodies out of the 333 eventually found.

The seas were rough, the fog was thick and it was heart-breaking work. Titanic First Class passenger dead were embalmed and put in coffins and stored to go back to Halifax. Second class dead were embalmed and put in canvas body bags and stored for Halifax. Third Class dead were put into canvas and buried at sea.

West took some photos and, at the time of my writing his main photo of a burial-at-sea taking place on board the ship is up for auction in the "West Country" and expected to fetch £5k.

Back at the time the crew took a great interest. They brought the bodies back home and there was a little boy who could not be identified, and was not claimed. The crew had been touched and insisted that he be brought back. The boy still had a pair of shoes on his feet.

There was a recent documentary on the BBC about the ships that made Britain great which featured the Mackay-Bennett, and I believe that many years after being buried, the little boy was finally identified, his DNA was matched with one of his descendants and he was named Sidney Leslie Goodwin aged 19 months at the time.

There was another officer on board the Mackay-Bennett and he kept a diary which included the tragic event. Some, or all, of that diary survived and it's in the National Maritime Museum in London. That officer's name was Fred Hamilton. Now, it's a small world, and I might be romancing just a little, but my brother's skipper on the H.M.S. Rodney when they went after the Bismarck was also a "Fred" Hamilton.

We had a good time back in Moncton. However, we were all a bit preoccupied because we were going home – albeit briefly for some. I remember thinking and hoping that the war would end soon and that *everybody* could go home. I wanted to settle down and live my life with Madge. I didn't think that there was anything wrong with a quiet happy life and I've been proved right – at least to my satisfaction.

As I strolled around in the freezing cold, even though I had no idea when we would be able to get married, I always had Madge on my mind. I knew the problems of getting hold of proper dresses for ladies back home, but clothing was not rationed in Canada and there were some very nice shops in Moncton. Strolling around I found a ladies outfitters with lots of lovely suits in the window and I decided that one of these suits in particular would suit Madge fine as a "going away" outfit after our wedding. Going away? Going away where, and when? Well, never mind about all that, I thought to myself. I knew her size, so I went inside to make the purchase, only to find out that they wouldn't sell the dress to me simply because it was window dressing. It was a display model. They would have to take it out of the window.

Take it out of the window? Change their display? At first I remember thinking to myself that perhaps I should say *"Don't you know there's a war on? Some of us are changing our whole lives every five minutes"*. The dress would be going on a ship that would be dodging U-Boats – again; but I held my tongue because I definitely wasn't going to war with the ladies in a ladies' outfitters. Not a chance. I'd rather get in the boxing ring with an instructor who was out to teach me a lesson.

Anyway, I soon realised that the ladies wanted to help. They kindly offered to make me another suit to my own choice of cloth and how lovely it turned out to be. It was even better than the one that was probably doomed to stay in the window forever. The new dress went fine with the matching gloves and shoes and with everything else I happily bought to complete the outfit. In fact, although I shouldn't say it, that suit gave good service for many years after we were married and demobbed.

Our time in Moncton passed quickly and soon we were catching the train the short distance to Halifax where our ship awaited us, and a cheer went up from the lads when we saw that it was none other than the good old *New Amsterdam* which had brought us safely to the USA in the first place. I don't know how many passengers were on board that time but as usual the ship was very busy. This time there was a large contingent of "Powerful Pierre" - French Canadian troops who were bound for the fighting that was still going on in Europe.

Once again, and thankfully, the journey was without incident and after six days we docked at Heysham in Lancashire. After disembarking we got a train to Harrogate. Our group's next posting was to Aldergrove in Northern Ireland, where we were to be part of Coastal Command. However, there was one major problem to be sorted out at Harrogate which was my missing kitbag. My heart sank. The bag hadn't arrived off the New Amsterdam in Heysham Dock. Now, it really wouldn't have been a big problem, and I would have gladly written it off if only the missing bag had not contained all the lovely things I had bought for Marjorie in Canada for the wedding. Resignation set in but after four days it just arrived. It was intact and I began to parcel it up for sending on to Marjorie at RAF St Athan. She told me that when the goodies arrived there it caused such a stir in her billet amongst her WAAF friends that they got her all dressed up and had a bit of a fashion parade. One of them even lent her a wedding dress for whenever the date could be fixed. However, the date was something that neither one of us had much control over.

Aldergrove, Northern Ireland - 1945

Aldergrove is on the east side of Lough Neagh, and on the west side there was another airfield where the US Air Force was doing a lot of training using Boston bombers. We used the lake for radar training with one part of it set up for an exercise where a pipe had been installed to look like a submarine periscope. Our planes would fly away from the periscope target for several miles and then they would turn around and come back in. It was then up to the radar ops to locate the target and guide the plane into an attack position. Our crew had the closest of shaves on one of these exercises. We were homing back onto the target and concentrating hard, when, from the opposite side and heading straight for us, came a US Sunderland flying boat doing the same exercise but coming from the opposite direction. Luckily both pilots were on their toes and swerved their respective planes away in the regulation way they had been taught. A disaster had been averted, but when we landed we never talked about it. We all acted as if nothing had happened at all. However, it wasn't just bravado. I was reminded about that "bit of luck" that the gunnery instructor at Pembrey had talked about when one of our trainees had almost shot down a plane and the pilot had landed and said nothing as he headed off to the pub. We'd had a close shave over the lake but my bit of luck didn't make me feel invincible. However, in a strange way it helped to reassure me that I'd had some luck to draw on.

At the beginning of April 1945 I was informed that I was due some leave, and I told Marjorie that our wedding could go ahead. Armed with this, Madge was now on a mission, which was something I was to see from here on many times in our life together. She worked so hard to get it done in time with only a week in which to arrange everything including her own leave, the church, a cake, and the thousand and one other things which all came together to make the big day complete. She did a great job and managed to get everything to work out fine.

Married life

We were married at St. George's church in Enfield Wash on the 21st April 1945. The warm spring weather was perfect and romance was in the air. Even today I still think about the number of young couples who were queuing at the church door to have their marriage sanctified. It was impossible to bring all our families and friends together. However, Harry Rodda, who was the half-brother of my old friend Wally Charles, and who could not join the forces because of health problems, was available for duty as best man.

Because of the shortage of time to arrange the wedding, we hadn't been able to book up anywhere for the honeymoon, but at the wedding Marjorie's Aunt Kath, whose husband was away in the army, just gave Marjorie the keys to her home in Stanmore in North London and went off to stay with Marjorie's mum and dad.

That week, our week on honeymoon in London, was blessed with the most gorgeous weather which really made it a time to remember. We spent the second week at my family's home in Strathaven, where despite a bit of April snow, it all went very well. My family had met Marjorie on that earlier occasion and they made her very welcome again. The time flew by. We came to the end of our first fourteen days together and then it was back to our separate places of work; Wales for Marjorie, and Ireland for me.

The end of the war in Europe was in sight but there was talk of some of our crews going to the Far East to become part of Transport Command, so now some of our training was done with that in mind. However, the end of the war arrived while we were still training and our crew made its final flight a couple of days after V.E. Day.

It was good and rewarding to look down on U-boats making their way to Londonderry to give themselves up. A number of them were then tied up along Lough Foyle, the inlet from the sea, and as members of Coastal Command we had the privilege of visiting the dock and going aboard one of them for a look around. Having crossed the Atlantic a couple of times, and been potential prey to a U-boat, I was interested to look around and especially to look out of a hunter's periscope.

Another reason I wanted to see Lough Foyle at Londonderry is because it was where Italo Balbo had landed with his formation of flying boats to great acclaim in July 1933 after it had flown over our house in Scotland. When they had passed overhead that day it had been a big moment for a young lad like me, and now I'd been places, too. I'd been taught how big planes like that stay up in the sky, and how to keep them up there. I stood by Lough Foyle and drank in the history I'd shared and seen. Balbo was dead. The official Italian line back in 1940 was that he had failed to give the correct recognition signals. His bit of luck had run out and he had been blown out of the sky by his own compatriots. I remembered the time when a trainee on our gunnery course at Pembrey nearly did the same thing to one of our airmen.

But now, and much faster than it took to join up, we were suddenly redundant aircrew. We all smiled and joked around as we quickly became out of work except for when we were wanted for the occasional important odd job which was great fun. When the Royal Family visited Northern Ireland and we lined the route on their way to Londonderry. Then there was the visit of General Eisenhower to receive the Freedom of Belfast, and the same for "Monty" - General Montgomery. There was also a parade for the Special Forces brigade called the Chindits, for their brave and selfless work in Burma and India. We did all of these things and, what with the rehearsals and the spit and polish, it kept us busy.

In essence we were clearing up after a war as many had done before over the centuries, breaking camp and going back to our villages. Back in camp there were chores to be done, like gathering equipment from around the airfield. The idea was to get it all properly stored and squared away but a lot of it just went missing. Nobody took it seriously. A diminutive WAAF officer was put in charge of us and the poor woman looked just ridiculous as she walked around smoking a pipe and ordering around our team of senior NCO's. Our accommodation had been the usual rows of long huts which now became a new little city of industry with most of its inhabitants working feverishly away making "something for the home". Most of these "somethings" were made with a wide range of pilfered materials from around the camp now all being put to good use. Everybody knew that most of it would be wasted or thrown away after the war.

Before long I got an early release classified as a Class B which meant that I was to replenish the national labour force; the idea was that well-trained and motivated servicemen would soon get on top of all the work that badly needed doing after the war years, especially all the new building projects suddenly going on around the country.

However, it wasn't as simple as that. I was already agitating to get back into civilian life, and while I was waiting to be officially discharged from the RAFVR (having been moved sideways on demob to the RAF Volunteer Reserve), I wrote to the last employer that I'd had before joining up to see if he had a job for me. Instead of just saying that he regretted having no vacancies and good luck, his reply informed me that giving me a job would mean paying off a man who was already working for him. As I knew the man he was talking about, it was a strange kind of response.

But, considering the number of servicemen being discharged at the time, the tone of the letter came as no real surprise to me. Maybe the government was pressuring small companies to take on more staff when they couldn't really afford to do so. However, I was still troubled by the singular nature of the reply because it was as if I had asked for someone else's job straight out. I put the letter in my pocket, realising that the world had got a little more thick-skinned.

But within weeks of my discharge the poor man whose job I had not asked for in the first place had a fatal accident. He had been starting up his lorry with a starting handle, but had neglected to take the vehicle out of gear. It had started, jumped forward and pinned him against a wall. When I heard about it the accident disturbed me out of all proportion. Not just because the man had been a kind and understanding sort, but because I would be filling a dead man's shoes. However, it wasn't the first time. Flying accidents had happened around us all the time in the war, like the bad one in Nassau where ten men got killed, and other men had to step in immediately, take over the job and get on with it.

My elder brother John of the Royal Navy

I wasn't the only one in our family who had gone to war. My elder brother John had also gone off to do his bit, but unlike me, he had joined the Royal Navy. When we were growing up John was my mentor and my pal, and as we grew older he became my confidant.

He was a clever young man who did as well at school as poor kids did in those days. Just like the rest of us he left school at fourteen and had to get himself a job. He found work in the tomato houses of which, unexpectedly, and given our northern situation in the British Isles, there were a good number in our area. These market gardens supplied both Glasgow and Edinburgh. You have to remember that in our part of the world - where people grew up on a legendary menu of mainly "meat and tatties" - a tomato had been an exotic fruit. John liked the work and was good at it but he was ambitious and, without waiting for a war to get under way, he joined the Royal Navy in 1938 at age eighteen

He did his training south of the border, at Devonport and it wasn't long before he was at sea on an armed merchant ship. By the time the war started in the autumn of 1939, John was well-prepared, having been trained in the hard business of gunnery. The Navy had always been the best since Admiral Nelson's day but the Germans had long caught up and John was involved in actions at sea that have gone down in history.

One action in particular was special and you always know when it's very special because sooner or later they make a film of it. In May 1941 John was on *HMS Rodney*, a Nelson Class battleship, named after another Admiral - Lord Rodney - and on convoy duty in the Atlantic when she was ordered to join in the hunt and attack on the fearsome German battleship the *Bismarck*. When the film was made the title summed it up completely: *Sink the Bismarck*.

The German battleship was supposed to be unsinkable, thanks to her exceptionally heavy armour plating and the biggest guns around. Her guns had enormous range and the ship was able to hit targets over the horizon.

The pride of the German navy, she had been launched in Hamburg by Hitler himself in 1939 and had lived up to her reputation in many a sea battle. However, the RN attack was well planned, efficient, and ruthless. The Bismarck had already been partially disabled by a torpedo launched from a Swordfish biplane which had damaged her rudder, but she was still a very dangerous entity. As battle commenced the attack brought the Rodney together with other battleships. My brother John manned one of the Rodney's 16 inch guns that helped blast the Bismarck into oblivion.

In life there are many strange coincidences and my brother's commanding officer on HMS Rodney was Frederick Hew George Dalrymple Hamilton - nicknamed Fred by his men. He was the son of – and let me be careful here and get it right - *the Honourable Colonel North de Coigny, of Bargany, Girvan, in Ayrshire, Scotland, and grandson of the 10th Earl of Stair.* Yes, quite a mouthful, but he was distantly related to the Duke of Hamilton for whom I worked as a pony boy.

John went on to serve as a petty officer on several ships, including HMS Capetown and HMS Newcastle from January 5th 1943 to May 29th 1945, often on the escort runs to Canada in the North Atlantic, taking care of troopships.

But perhaps most important of all the duties he carried out was something that affected him greatly in the post war period and in civilian life. John took part in many of those dangerous convoys up into the Arctic to Murmansk and Archangel, whereby we supplied essential goods and armaments to keep the Russians' war effort going against the Nazis. These convoys were constantly attacked by U-boats that often hunted up there in those dreaded wolf packs, and thousands of sailors died in those bitter waters, where the average life expectancy before hypothermia killed you was just a matter of a couple of minutes. Many sailors who were not blown to bits in ammunition-carrying ships died in those bitter waters. Fatalities from those kinds of open-water deaths start with the shock of being plunged into the icy water itself, followed immediately by a massive physical panic reaction, and the chronic inability to hold the breath.

There was also - it was little known about at the time - a cause of cold water death which is called Rescue Collapse. This is caused by pulling people out from their vertical position in the water which is a necessary but often final and fatal challenge to both heart and brain. (Source of information on open water death: Rosemary Kingsland from her book *Savage Seas*. (Boxtree Books and Granada TV.)

Many Russians who lived through WW2 - a war that the Russians themselves called the Great Patriotic War - had no idea until quite recently that we had supplied them with anything at all. Stalin's version of the facts of WW2 concentrated mainly on Stalin himself - the hero. Communist Party propaganda had convinced the Russians that they had done it all themselves. Let's face it, history has shown your average Russian that it wasn't prudent to dispute Stalin's version of *anything*.

Despite our different military careers, and the fact that John was often away at sea, we tried to keep up with each other. Based at a naval establishment John had met a young lady who was a naval nurse and a wonderful friendship had developed between them that he hoped would lead to marriage. In 1942 John had arranged for me to spend the weekend at this young lady's home and meet her family. At the time I was in Lincolnshire and, since it was an opportunity to catch up and perhaps hear plans for a wedding, I got a weekend pass to travel to St. Albans to meet the Smith family who gave me a lovely welcome.

Mr Smith was what we called a boffin. He was an inventor doing secret work for the War Office, and sometimes doing it in his back garden in St Albans - where there were two O.P.'s (Observation Posts) disguised as real trees. The trees were man-made of course, but they looked very real and were intended to conceal snipers. On the Saturday Mr Smith invited John and me to accompany him for a drive into London where he had some business to attend to at the War Office in Whitehall. On the way we stopped off at the De Havilland aircraft factories at Watford where he was obviously well-known. Some of the most iconic planes that helped us win the war were built there including Spitfires. I found it all fascinating, especially a plane that appealed to many aircraft watchers which was the wooden wonder called the Mosquito. It packed quite a punch and seemed ridiculous given that they were built mostly of balsa wood – the hobby shop type of wood that you make model planes out of by gluing all the bits together.

In January 1943 Hermann Göring, chief of the Luftwaffe, was reported to have gone into one of his famous rants, - the kind of tirade where his air force problems were always someone else's fault. He had shouted: *"In*

1940 I could fly as far as Glasgow in most of my aircraft, but not now! It makes me furious when I see the Mosquito. I turn green and yellow with envy."

Meanwhile, in London in 1942 Mr Smith the boffin (I've often wondered if Smith was his real name) talked about a couple of projects he was involved in, while at the same time asking us questions and also inviting suggestions for these projects. It was my kind of weekend although I've always been sad at the fact that, for some reason, John's romance with Mr. Smith's daughter did not end in marriage. However, our weekend with them was a welcome and fascinating break for both of us.

After the war was over, like me, John had also returned home to Scotland, at least for a while, and we shared some good yarns. John was a navy man through and through and he stayed on in the service. When John was asked about something that had happened in the war - perhaps something that he still considered secret - he would smile, slowly bring his forefinger to his lips and say, "that's secret talk".

John stayed on in the Royal Navy long after WW2 finished and by then I was working all hours and I didn't see my parents - who were keepers of the family news – as much as I would have liked to. Sadly, John and I just lost touch. In his later years he was not in the best of health. The rigours and the anxiety of war, especially serving on the Arctic Convoys, seemed to have drained him and, like so many old hands, he took to drink.

He became introverted and died of pneumonia at sixty-five alone in a hospital in Greenock. However, I have the satisfaction of knowing that he was laid to rest with a proper stone in the family lair in Strathaven Cemetery beside his grandfather and other Leggates.

Civvy Street - 1945 and beyond

When I was in the forces, like most young men at that time, I had looked to the future and my ambitions for peacetime. These ambitions were very simple and straightforward: I just wanted to be settled down and to bring up a family. The family would be educated and give us a lot of pleasure in their achievements when they took their place in the world. Madge and I had married just a few weeks prior to the war ending in Europe. We now had a lot of catching up to do in our normal, everyday lives beyond the war. Finally, when both our discharges were completed, we made our start on fulfilling these ambitions.

Getting down to life on Civvy Street again took some adjusting. I had gone into the RAF as a nineteen year old and was now coming home a married man of twenty-three. Marjorie and I were lucky to get a room at my parents' home, which was very convenient because I wanted to get a job close to Strathaven. I still had some very good connections in the building industry in the area.

Meanwhile, Marjorie's sometime name of Madge had quickly overtaken the use of Marjorie – except for Sundays. For her, the main problem was adjusting to the Scottish way of life, and she had all my family to contend with. I knew that this would be a challenge, but with her ability to get on with people easily, I was confident that she would begin to make lasting friendships and win people over. The years she had spent in the WAAF, mixing in with girls from many different ways of life, helped her to see all different points of view. She had been very popular with her WAAF-mates and so I felt that, although there would be adjustments all round, it would all be all right in the end.

And then suddenly there were problems. Now, over the years, I have given a lot of thought to what happened and what might have been. We had arrived in Strathaven with high hopes as a new married couple and that was fine, but on the domestic front at least, it all started to go wrong. After an initial period when I was welcomed home from the war, my parents, and especially my mother, soon showed that they did not want to share their home with a young Englishwoman. I was their son and as far as they were concerned I belonged there, but in their eyes my wife was an outsider. I have agonised over what happened and I have tried to be honest. This is how I remember it:

I had always helped out since I was a kid. I did my chores and from the age of eleven I always contributed cash to the family's weekly income from paper rounds and milk rounds and more. After I left school I worked full time. I didn't think twice about contributing. I didn't resent it. Why would I? Life was life and you helped out. I didn't smoke, never have, and I usually take no more than a single dram of whisky at celebrations, but those are simply my choices. I don't preach to anybody else about their own lifestyle choices. When I came home on leave from the RAF I was generous to the household in general. Everything was just fine on a visit, but when I returned home to the family with my wife it was different.

Essentially, Madge was thrown in at the deep end. It was an unintentional sink-or-swim, and it didn't work. We had visited before and it had been fine, but suddenly Madge had no job to go to as she had in the WAAF's. She couldn't get out of the way. There was nowhere she needed to be in the daytime and she was acutely aware of that. It may have been as simple as nobody having enough space to themselves, but the atmosphere in the home turned icy and downright unfriendly. On occasions, Madge asked my mother what the problem was – hoping it was something she could fix – but she got no explanation in return.

Madge tried all she knew, but she was hurting. She tried to help by taking care of my disabled youngest brother Richard. She thought that, in time – and with time always being a great healer – maybe things would improve and she would be accepted.

Meanwhile she took Richard off for long walks that often lasted for a good part of the day. She went off around the countryside where I had roamed as a boy. Getting out of the house for long periods was all right in fine weather, but not when it rained or was cold.

As for me, I was also under some pressure. I had always been busy in the RAF but now I was just one of the thousands of jobless men trying to get back on their feet in a depressed economy. I was hoping it would all work out. I looked everywhere for work and an opportunity eventually came along, with an expanding company that were based only four miles away. They'd been given contracts for thousands of new homes in Glasgow and Lanarkshire to meet the demand for huge numbers of returning servicemen and women. I started work with them at my old trade of joiner and I was a little bit rusty after four years away from real joinery. However, I was given a lot of help and consideration from my new workmates on the workshop floor, which soon got me back in the groove again. Many of them had been in the forces and were relishing the challenge of settling into new homes with their wives and a bright new future.

After about a year with the company one of my workmates, a guy called Stan, suggested that the pair of us should start our own business and I readily agreed. Looking back, it was definitely a bit of a hasty decision. I think I must have felt a bit unsettled, or maybe I was just in a hurry. Whatever it was, Stan was a bit of a card, but he was good company, and he persuaded me. Through one of his contacts we managed to get the use of an empty shop which was quite roomy and then we just started working away without really giving much thought as to what we were getting into.

Christmas 1946 was coming up and although timber was still in short supply, we decided to make some toys which were also in short supply. Our thinking was good because with toy-making we could use up any old bits and pieces of wood – in fact, all the off-cuts that nobody wanted. It wasn't a bad plan at all and we managed to make enough money to keep us going. I was running a small business and able to keep my head above water by not only making toys but making small bits of furniture and getting a few small jobs around the town.

Stan and I carried on into early 1947 but we could never get our hands on enough timber to really make things work and, seeing no prospect of a fast improvement in our situation, Stan got impatient and baled out. He said there was good money to be made working on the new hydroelectric dams being constructed in the North of Scotland. We remained good friends but Stan was always getting into scrapes.

Working on the dam projects he had to live away in work-camp accommodation up in the hills, which, unfortunately, not only left his wife to take care of the home – but on her own. One day he got an unexpected opportunity for a quick visit home and upon arrival he opened up the door and found a completely empty house. It was the shock of his life. There was absolutely nothing in the house. "No wife, no furniture, no nothing", as Stan put it.

It must have felt like a silent movie starring Charlie Chaplin with that old maudlin piano tinkling away in the background, and then it got worse. As he wandered around in a daze opening doors and cupboards and only finding "more nothing", there was a knock at the door and there stood a gentleman who cheerfully announced that he'd come to collect the furniture. "Come on in," said Stan.

They soon came to the obvious conclusion that his wife had sold all the furniture – at least twice as it later turned out, before making her escape with whoever she'd escaped with. Stan did all kinds of things after that but I think he lacked application. He was good fun when we met up but a bit of a butterfly flitting here and there and never settling for long. At one time he got himself a pub and a gun dog and had a lucky escape one morning when the dog trod on the trigger and almost blew him away. After a life filled with scrapes, Stan died peacefully behind the wheel of his car - literally. He had taken a new wife shopping and while she popped into a shop, he waited. On her return she found him dead.

Now I tell you this story about Stan because back while I was still working with him halfway through 1946, Madge and I had found out that we were to become parents. This caused me to sit down and have a think about life. I would soon have even more responsibility, and the situation at home was not good at all. When the time came for Madge to go to the hospital at Belshill - a suburb of Glasgow, some ten miles away - the weather was wild up in Lanarkshire with many of the roads blocked with snow.

The ambulance driver had to try several routes before he found a road that was open to traffic but John, our first born, came into this world in March 1947 with no problem at all and then mother and son progressed at a good pace. Visiting the maternity hospital was not easy with many roads blocked and on each trip I would usually have to make a different detour. In the end it all turned out well with both mother and bairn home after a week. However, a new routine had to be set up, not easy to do in my parents' overcrowded and unhappy dwelling. Something had to be sorted out.

1947 turned out to be one of the worst winters on record in the UK with thousands of animals dead in the fields and even hardy moorland ponies dying wholesale of cold and starvation. People were cut off without electricity and the extreme weather persisted for months, causing many people and small businesses, including shops, to lose their income. Everybody struggled. I struggled and made just enough cash to contribute. We all waited for the weather to improve.

While we waited we began to think about a home of our own. We talked and we dreamed a bit about the future and I think it helped because with three of us now shoe-horned into a tight space, it led to an even deeper freeze for Madge. As a young mother with a first baby, she found it hard to cope with the stress, but cope she did and if possible, I loved her even more.

Then, one night, and with the strain still unremitting, I overheard Mum and Dad talking. They were discussing the possibility of buying a house in town. Incredibly, we were all dreaming the same sort of dream. I wasn't listening or eavesdropping but I could hear every word they were saying clearly. They wanted to buy the property for cash but they were a little bit short of what was required. For working class people, laying out cash for a house wasn't as amazing as it sounded. Sixty or seventy years ago property in many areas was relatively cheap and many people saved hard for a home of their own.

Without hesitation or any pretence that I hadn't heard everything they had been saying, I went and joined them and I said that Marjorie and I both still had our final payments to come from the RAF and however much we got it was theirs to use if they wanted. They accepted immediately. I sighed with relief. It was a great solution because my parents had been short of what was needed and, on its own, our RAF gratuity wouldn't have bought very much. Combined with what they had, it made all the difference.

Marjorie and I were happy the cash was put to good use and of course we hoped that this gesture - made without any stipulations or strings attached - would not only lead to a new and less crowded home, but would help to resolve things.

It wasn't to be. After a short time in the new house in North Street it was clear that the old atmosphere had simply been transferred from one house to another. Despite being very short of money and now with no gratuities to draw on, I felt we had little alternative other than to get a place of our own.

At that time, the general way to get a first-time home was to make enquiries at the local authority to see if there was any possibility of renting a council house from them. I visited our local councillor to get some information on what to do and find out what was happening in the area. It was a shock. He reckoned that I would probably have to wait about seven years for a vacancy. Seven years? Less than seven seconds after he'd told me this I had switched off thinking about renting and made up my mind to buy a home - just about any home that I could afford so that I could be independent and not have to rely on others.

At this time a local lawyer had asked me to do a few jobs in his home and while I was working there I took the opportunity of asking him if he could let me know when he had a suitable property for sale and at a price that was reasonable. I knew that he often had properties passing across his desk, and he readily agreed that he would tip me off when he thought one of them was suitable. I told him I would prefer an old property that needed fixing, and soon a house I knew would suit us very well came along. That's when our life changed, and it changed because we were then in a similar position to where my parents were when they were short of the whole amount they needed to buy a house. So I asked my father if they could help, but he just answered with a curt "no".

With that, I think the matter was closed. I never found out if his answer had been a straight refusal to help, or whether they were unable to help at that particular time and were embarrassed. Sadly, there was nothing else said. There was no more discussion when all I desperately needed was a few words of explanation.

It's possible that my parents simply didn't want Madge around at all and were hoping that we might decide to move to London and move in with Madge's parents. Perhaps they thought that if we moved away it would resolve the strange rift by itself. Maybe they thought we would all come together again sometime in the future and come to accept that a parting had been the best thing for everybody at the time. I don't know – will never know.

I have also wondered whether, unbeknown to me, my brother John had ever brought his girlfriend back home. I have wondered whether he had brought the Smith's daughter back to Strathaven. Whether the girl I saw when John and I visited them for a weekend had felt the same chilly wind as Madge?

It was painful. I wondered whether that's why John's romance had come to an end. Was that what happened? John had never mentioned a word to me about the reasons for the end of his romance. There had been no hint that Mr Smith the inventor or his wife had disapproved of John or me in any way when we had stayed with them for the weekend. I wondered if that was the main reason that John had stayed on in the Royal Navy after the war. I wondered if in his quiet moments he had got depressed about losing the girl he'd loved.

But wondering about possibilities was not good for me. I'll never know now. A lot of explanations were possible and, over the course of time, Madge and I had wondered and worried away at all of them. In the end, we had simply decided that we would probably have to find our friends "outwith" - which is a Scottish way of saying "outside the family". It was a decision that I was always sorry that I'd had to make. I still fall into thinking about it, and I have to push the sad feelings away, but I know they will never go away completely. I have to stop and do something to take my mind off it. The lesson I learned was simple yet it was a hard one and heart-breaking; I found that it's easier to fall out with family than with friends. Sometimes there's no road home, but like Sir Harry Lauder sang, you've got to *"keep right on to the end of the road"*.

I had told Mr Nunn the lawyer that I'd have the house and I was determined. Within three weeks, with the help of an overdraft at the bank and the assistance of a good lady customer of mine who stood as a guarantor, Madge and I were settled into our first home. Married life began in earnest. The property consisted of four one room and kitchen apartments and two attic apartments. We began by taking one room and a kitchen and one attic apartment for ourselves, and letting out the rest to repay the bank. Within six months the loan was cleared and I got down to seriously improving our accommodation.

That was the start of about forty years repairing and renovating the entire building in between earning a living. Today, sixty years or more on, it stands as a fine town house where our son David and his family live. From 1947 our family had increased from John onwards until we had five boys. They were all different, with different interests. As they grew up and went to school they made their own chums. The result of five boys all having their own chums meant that our home was often like a beehive with all of them coming and going. We kept a very open house and looking back on those times it would be difficult to count the children who came through the door. Some lads were even brought to Madge to be looked after while their mums got on with other things. John's appearance in the snows of `47 was followed in 1950 by Stephen, William in 1951, David in 1953 and, six years later in 1959, Andrew completed the team.

Being the only child for the first three years John had the privilege of two doting parents concentrating on his particular upbringing. I have to say that he showed very early signs of being exceptionally bright, but then, as they came along, so did his brothers. We were truly blessed and there was a quickness and good manners about them that, as parents, pleased us as we went along. All the boys had the full attention of Madge and me with their education and upbringing. I had my rules about bringing up a family, which were mainly to lead by example and, as far as possible to treat them all the same. This was always going to be a hard rule to maintain considering the differences in all children's natures, but it seemed to work and I have often seen other parents struggle - parents with maybe only one or two who have had more troubles than we had with five boys. All of them did well with their school work. They were also boy scouts, with the pleasure of going away and camping on home ground in Scotland and on the Continent. They travelled to Germany, France and Switzerland and I think travelling was a great aid to their education and in particular to their confidence.

Stephen, our second son was born in 1950. He was also very good at school and after he left he got a job in banking, but eventually banking didn't suit him. He didn't let it get him down and took an assortment of different jobs until he found something that suited him. He drove buses for the Glasgow Corporation and enjoyed it so much that he carried on doing it until he was fifty when he took early retirement to spend more time with his wife, Mary.

William was born in 1951 and carried on the family tradition of working hard at school and doing well. He also tried out several jobs before eventually settling down with the John Menzies Group - a very well-known and respected concern which had a lot of shops all over the country and sold books and magazines as well as a host of other allied goods. He then went on to work for Ipswich Town Football Club – nicknamed the Tractor Boys – and later moved on to work in management with Ipswich Council. The coming of the computer age interested him greatly and he became something of a self-taught computer wizard. William has settled in Ipswich with his wife Vivien. In his spare time he gardens. He's passionate about it, which is perhaps something he inherited from his mother.

Our son David, who lives nearby, has always been very helpful, especially in the long period of battling to keep Madge from as much discomfort as possible after her accident. He also applied himself to the books and did really well at school. He was awarded a Dux Medal at Strathaven Academy and then went on to higher education. However, before long he decided to quit education and to dedicate himself to work in places like the Doctor Barnardo's Homes for orphaned and abandoned children and such. This was a very unselfish thing to do. In fact, after he got married to Elizabeth and their family began to arrive, they jointly made another big decision and came to an arrangement that was still somewhat 'before its time'. They decided that David would stay at home and run the house, and therefore Elizabeth could carry on working as a science teacher. It made sense, and it worked. Later, after their own boys were old enough, David took a job as a local park ranger in Strathaven Park. After his family, Strathaven Park is David's pride and joy.

There are really no big gaps between first four boys, but six years between David and Andrew, our youngest. Once again the lad did well at school. He was a bright spark and went to Glasgow University where he took a degree in law – an LLB, and it's good to have a lawyer in the family. However, Andrew is also a qualified accountant. He now lives in Hertfordshire with his wife Joanne, and they have a thriving accountancy practice and financial advisory business.

Our Leggate boys have given Marge and me the great gift of 9 grandchildren and, to date, 4 great grandchildren. The Leggate Clan continues to thrive.

I make no bones about it: education is a serious matter. I like to read and I read a bit about Sir Harry Lauder's life. For many years he was Strathaven's most famous resident and when he died in 1950 the shops all closed on the day of his funeral. His life story was in all the papers and it was fascinating. Now I like to know about people and about the thinking behind their success, and so did Madge, especially when they come from humble beginnings. I also liked the fact that, during the war, Harry Lauder used to go down to the docks in Glasgow when food ships arrived from America, and thank them personally.

Harry Lauder's mum was named Isabella and she was born to a family from the Black Isle. She had lost her husband early but was determined that, despite the family's sudden reduced circumstances - she and the seven children were taken in by her brother - her children would not only get a proper education, but an education that, if necessary, she would push to the limit with her limited resources.

Mrs Lauder was determined that Harry - who was the eldest child - would not just leave school as early as eleven or twelve to work fulltime, as was the custom back then. She gave it some thought and came up with a compromise. She arranged a part-time job at a mill so that he could continue to study until he was sixteen. She realised that the more schooling children got, the better equipped they were for life. If she could set an education precedent, the other children would follow. With Harry it didn't quite work out the way she thought, but in a way it did.

Harry Lauder didn't take the normal road when he eventually left school. He didn't become something like a colliery manager in Hamilton - which was what his mother's own father did for a living - or become a teacher or a professional man as his mother had initially hoped. In a way he did take on the world on his own terms because he used his education and knowledge to write songs and carve out and manage a very lucrative business career for himself in show business.

Harry Lauder was the first Scottish artist to sell a million records. His understanding of life and its joys and trials endeared him not only to the nation but to a worldwide audience. He made no less than twenty two visits to the USA where he travelled around in his *own railroad car*. At one stage he was earning the equivalent of £12,000 per night and was the highest paid entertainer in the world. Winston Churchill said that Harry rendered measureless service to the Scots race and to the British Empire.

Madge had been to a really good school in London before getting an office job and then signing up as a WAAF, whilst I had been a pony boy for the local Duke. As I've said, I also read a lot and went on to get a good training as a mechanic in the RAF. So, as you can imagine, we were both keen that our sons should not only get some good schooling, but that we would take advantage of the best opportunities that presented themselves, and would help other opportunities along with a helpful kick up the backside. We were hard on our boys about study and homework. Madge would always make sure that all homework was done before they left the house in the morning, and she was always there and ready to help out.

A time came when an opportunity arose, when our son John had obviously reached the limits of our local academy at Strathaven and we wanted him to go to the advanced and respected Hamilton Academy to complete his education. Everything was in place for this to happen but the Strathaven headmaster saw it differently. It was apparent that this man looked unfavourably on upstarts with working-class parents who wanted their children to have the chance to move beyond their status in life. He had decided that I was just a joiner with a family and would not sanction John to go to the county academy in Hamilton.

Madge went to see him. They had a chat about his decision but to no avail. The man wouldn't budge. So I took up the cudgel and went to see Mister Pompous Headmaster myself. I made my feelings clear in a forthright way and the man backed down. He reversed his decision. The result was that not only did John get his place, but four other bright pupils from working class families in the school also benefitted by being "allowed" to go on to Hamilton Academy.

If I'd had a business card in my wallet that day with my name and telephone number on it, the job description underneath my name might have read *Opinions Changed*.

Enough said, and I have to commend all the other parents who supported us during this time and the teachers who expressed disgust at the behaviour of their senior in a strange episode in Scottish education. The headmaster retired in due course and years later at Buckingham Palace as I watched Prince Charles pin a Commander of the British Empire insignia on John, I remembered the man – but not fondly.

In fact, if the truth be known, Hamilton Academy has a history of being quite daring in its own way, too. It remains the only professional British football club ever to have been formed from what was just the school team. Their colours were originally – wait for it - 'cerise and French grey', if you please, which were the racing colours of the Duke. The club is called Hamilton Academicals and was formed in 1874 by the Rector James Blacklock. The name is often abbreviated on the terraces and the pubs to the "Accies" (with a hard 'c').

The team has had some success over the years, reaching the Scottish Cup Final twice only to get second prize both times, being narrowly beaten on separate occasions by both Glasgow super teams – that's Rangers, and their arch-rivals Celtic. Those cup final defeats were thirty years apart. Quite recently they have also enjoyed a three year run in the Premier League in Scotland, and are currently back in the top flight for the forthcoming 2014/15 season. They will soon kick off the new season against Inverness Caledonian Thistle. What great Scottish names. It does your heart proud just to see a fixture like that *on paper*.

Madge stayed at home bringing up our growing family, while I made my living on building sites. I worked for an employer until 1972 when an opportunity came along to become self-employed. This meant that I had an arrangement to hire myself out (along with any other help I needed) to a big company from the North of England which had expanded into Scotland to a number of new locations. It was hard-earned money but I stuck it out and in the end I felt that I had profited from it in a number of ways. The top man in the building company was an ex-professional footballer called Barnes. At that time they had one hundred and eighty building sites on the go throughout the UK, and Barnes travelled around the sites in his Rolls Royce with his henchmen. He would often arrive at one of his sites around seven in the morning and then he and his team would sit in the Rolls at a good surveillance spot and watch what went on at the site at the start of the working day.

As was my habit I was early to work one morning and I started to lay out the material for my day's work, unaware that I was being observed. After I'd started work, Barnes and his men appeared and, quite unbelievably accused me of being a thief. Why? Because I was there so early, they said. They shook their heads and said that nobody comes in early in the building trade. Therefore I was obviously up to no good. I just looked at Barnes and told him that if there was any more of that kind of talk he'd have to put up his fists. His henchmen got a bit upset at their boss being spoken to like that, but Barnes understood it very quickly, and peace prevailed.

In fact I continued to work for the company for about four years until they started to have serious cash flow problems. Nobody really knew what was going on except Barnes. A Receiver was appointed on behalf of the banks who reckoned the debt was about £40 million - a huge amount of money back then. In fact the company had so many building sites with jobs going on here there and everywhere - and with a lot of builders on the new self-employed (often abused) arrangement with the inland revenue - that it took two years to sort out. Finally the Receivers worked out that the company was not trading insolvently (which is a serious offence) but was worth £80 million. I smiled when I read that in the papers. I like a man who works hard and creates a lot of employment. I also know that any man like me who is up early and on site at seven is probably a man who is driven. Barnes was a hard case and he might have arrived in a flash Roller, but lazy he wasn't.

I have always been driven in my own way, and as I've also said I wanted to lead my sons by example. They knew that I went to work and put in a good day. That fact was not lost on them. As the years passed, I gained a reputation as a worker and the kind of builder who was also a problem-solver. I began to get a good deal of private work. I have never had a Rolls Royce but I was as driven as Barnes the Builder. I was the ex-RAF aircraft mechanic. I kept fit and I took care of business.

Madge's parents Steve and Sophie were a lovely couple and I counted myself lucky to have them as in-laws. Down the years we often visited each other and went back and forth between Strathaven and London. I had got to know them well. We were like many families of that era who had been through wars. Steve had really been through it. He'd been through many bad experiences in WW1. The poor man had been gassed and shot at in the trenches. He had survived Gallipoli, contracted malaria. Then when he came home in 1918 he had to scrabble around looking for work. He had tramped the roads and slept in hedgerows along with others.

When we played cards, I used to look at him across the table and wonder what had gone through his mind when, in 1939, barely twenty years after the end of WW1, we were going to do it all over again. Back in 1918, almost before you could re-fold the newspaper with its headlines announcing "Victory" - and put it back down on the table - the bombs were exploding around you again. Britain was again fighting for its life, and this time his daughter gets her own version of call-up papers, with a choice of options, and she's off and joining the WAAF's. What was life all about?

It's a strange fact that perennial questions like *What's it all about?* and *What's going on?* can only be explained by someone like a music-hall performer. There was a man who summed it all up by answering those questions with another question. He used to shamble on stage dressed in a tatty old WW1 uniform and cap, stand in the middle of the stage and look mournfully out at the audience shielding his eyes. The pianist would play a WW1 tune, the crowd would smile in expectation and he'd milk it. Then he would take out a sheet of crumpled paper and a stub of pencil and he'd lick the pencil and screw up his face in painful thought. Only then would he speak for the common man as he pretended to write his first line: *Dear, Mother, is it worth it?* And the crowd would erupt because so many of them had been there.

My own brother John had been destroyed by the war just as surely as if his ship had been blown up in the Arctic by a torpedo from a U-Boat. His life was ruined. If he had come home safe he might have married and grown tomatoes. More to the point we could have grown old together. It wasn't to be.

Around 1972 Steve and Sophie were beginning to need a little help with life. By then they had retired to Norfolk and were living on their own. Madge began to worry about her mother's growing lack of mobility because she had bad arthritis. After talking it over Madge and I decided to make a flat for her parents in part of our property in Strathaven. There was space on the ground floor and so we had an architect friend design a plan to put the available rooms together and create a flat with bathroom and kitchenette. Once the drawings were passed by the council planning committee I got on with the job and as soon as the flat was ready they sold their house in Norfolk and moved to Scotland, where they settled in comfortably. As Madge was their one and only child, it was a great relief to have them close by so that she could be there to give them whatever help they required and all the family could visit and entertain them. They loved a game of whist and on many evenings we would go down and play.

We had them with us for about six years until Sophie died. Steve survived her by only eight days. They had always reckoned on going together, and that's how it was.

When new families came to live in our street, Madge, who was a great church worker, would pay them an informal visit and, if there were children that might be recruited for the West Church Sunday school she'd have them. She'd often be seen heading for the church with a gaggle of new recruits. An understanding of the Ten Commandments never hurt. Some folks got to know Madge as "Mrs West Church", and in her time as an Elder as well as the holder of many other posts to do with the running of the church, she became very popular.

Another local family and close friends of ours were John and Jean Ness. They were the greatest fundraisers that the town of Strathaven have ever known. They must have raised at least £500,000 in their time. One particular charity they put a great deal of time into was the Erskine Hospital for disabled ex-servicemen which was also a cause that was close to my heart. The main event to raise money was an annual ball which was held in Strathaven Town Hall. They ran it for forty years, finally ending with a superb gala dinner dance. Madge and I generally had a part to play. Madge did a lot of baking and I helped to set up the events. There were also a great number of generous local people who donated raffle prizes to raise cash. Interestingly, John Ness' hobby was tapestry and he always had a piece underway. He turned out so many beautiful pieces that on occasion I helped him set up exhibitions of his work. We would take the whole church and show them off and raise cash for charity. People like John and Jean Ness had a lifetime commitment to hard work in their bones.

Meanwhile I never really retired. Even now friends still call me up when they require a helping hand with some of their DIY home jobs. I put this longevity down to the simple fact that I have always kept fit. I had a very pleasant surprise during 1990 when I was asked to build a stage on which

Her Majesty Queen Elizabeth would make a speech for an official opening ceremony of a new building project in East Kilbride and I was invited to attend the ceremony itself. I was also able to take a few photographs of the Queen and her companions as they walked through the new Plaza. When I was eighty I got a visit from a friend in the building trade who was beginning to have health problems and unable to cope with a building job at a golf range which he was unable to finish. It gave me great pleasure. That kind of thing was always happening.

By 1992, when Madge and I turned 70, we were on the lookout for another home which would be more suitable in our advancing years. We had mentioned this to the family and, before long, our son David saw an advert for a house locally which might fit the bill. It did and it had a view right onto our public park. It was only a ten minute walk into town to the medical centre, the church and all the shops we would ever need. The decision to buy it took no time at all. Within two weeks all the paperwork was in order and we moved in with a bit of help from friends who provided all the transport.

In 1995 Madge and I arrived at our golden wedding anniversary. We seemed to have come a long way from the day we had met at that dance back in St. Athan, in South Wales. We had not even thought about how we would celebrate fifty years as a couple but one Saturday afternoon Madge was doing some work in the kitchen and I was browsing through the paper when I saw an advert for a trip on the QE2. It was departing from Greenock. It was the first time the liner would sail from Scotland and, having once sailed to New York from Greenock under slightly different circumstances in 1944, I decided that it would be wonderful to do it again with Madge. Another strange coincidence was that back in 1944 I had crossed the Atlantic in early September and the QE2 was scheduled to make the crossing at the same time of year. This time, I would see the Manhattan skyline from the deck of a luxurious ocean liner instead of from a troop ship loaded with ten thousand souls. I liked the idea so much that I had a few words with Madge and within the hour we were booked up. The trip was marvellous.

Our retirement years were very happy, but on 3rd of October 1997 Madge had a very bad accident. On the way back from a coffee morning to raise funds for the Macmillan Nurses at the local church hall she was hit by a car.

After her coffee morning stint Madge had set off for home and did a little shopping along the way. Suddenly a car just swerved across the road and crashed into her, sending her into the air. She had bounced off another car's windscreen before she hit a wall and fell back to earth. She ended up jammed between a car and a house wall as local residents came running from their homes to see what they could do. They made her as comfortable as possible till the ambulance arrived and the remarkable thing was that during the time immediately after the smash, Madge did not lose consciousness and was giving out phone numbers where our son David and I could be found.

David was on the scene in about five minutes and went with her to Hairmyres Hospital at East Kilbride where the emergency team went to work on her. Both legs were broken and the left one was causing the surgeon a lot of concern. He had to decide very quickly about whether to amputate or try to save it. After a survey of the damage he made up his mind that it could be saved. According to David, Madge never stopped chatting between the crash and the operating table.

"That evening I got a call from my brother David to tell me about the accident, to warn me that Mum might be dead by morning, and to say that we should fly up as soon as possible. We arrived and Mum was visibly in a very sorry state and drowsy from the medication. However, on the way into the hospital I had stopped to buy some flowers and – because I thought it might be a long vigil – I'd got a copy of the Hamilton Advertiser. As it was around the time of the new school year the paper had made a little feature and, by coincidence they had put a photo of the new school entrants to the Strathaven Primary School next to an old photo of new school entrants back in my year at Crosshill School in 1952. I chatted away and told Mum about the feature in the paper and I showed it to her. I said to her that I could not remember the names of many of my classmates. That's when Mum took another look before reeling off the names of all these small kids – and then she reeled off many of their wives or husbands and some of their children's names. In spite of the dreadful accident and

the medications, her sharp mind and near-perfect memory were pretty much intact "

John Leggate. 2014

During her three month stay in hospital all the church ministers from all the various denominations visited to have a few words with her and sometimes a prayer. A staff doctor who had been on duty when Madge was brought in came to her bedside after a few days on the recovery ward to see how she was coping. Madge said he told her that there had been a big X against her name in the early stages but that she had been rejected by both heaven and hell and this was the reason why she was still on the planet. Many of the hospital staff had a good sense of humour. It was great for morale. Another doctor at Hairmyres, who was not only a cancer surgeon but a church friend of Madge's, made a point of visiting her each day before he went home after his shift in the operating theatre. Madge was truly grateful for it all. The A & E team had done a great job at the start. The care continued long after Madge was allowed home to a great welcome from the family and a host of friends. After that countless visitors arrived every day and at times our house became more like a café than a home.

Madge had a leg in plaster for the next three years, and during that time she also had three bone grafts and some other injuries attended to. It may sound a little pious but with our faith we didn't allow the accident and its aftermath to blight our lives. Thanks to all our wonderful family and close friends, we coped well. We were lucky that our son David and his family lived in the town and they were always on the lookout for ways to help out. They were there, as they are always there when the occasion arises, along with our other sons and their families who live farther away. We got the best of attention from all of them. It was a time to sit back and rest up and a time to hear about all the family news and to see all the young ones and find out how they were getting on.

Around that time a good friend of mine, Frank Cole, who worked as a plumber, and who was one of the first people to respond when Madge was injured, became a regular visitor. Frank was a real character and a boon to our community. He was not only a good fundraiser but an eccentric one who tackled just about anything that might raise some cash for charity, and

I mean *anything*. This often entailed activities - things like climbing *all* of Scotland's two hundred mountains that were over two thousand feet high, competing in *all* of the British marathons and cycling *all* the way back from Land's End down in Cornwall to John O' Groats up in Scotland. Another of Frank's roles for charity was a strange marathon-type run which started 16,000 feet up on Mount Everest and then went "downhill" from there - in more ways than one. Frank got lost twice on the way down but survived when others perished.

Frank loved to fish and he often brought Madge rainbow trout. Only one fish about every two weeks or so but it still went on for ten years. I tell this story because everyone at the fishing spot knew the reason for Frank's fishing expeditions and when he caught one a great trout-shout would go up and along the bank that he had caught *Madge's Fish!*

Madge had eventually been able to get around and even to do some light gardening, an activity which had always been a passion of hers. I put in some raised beds to make gardening possible and she spent many hours outdoors in all weathers. There were always new innovations that came along and helped to get things done a little easier, and make life simpler. As time passed, she needed help twenty-four hours a day, having lost all ability to walk and to get about the house on her own.

Gradually, my life became focussed on looking after Madge, and that was fine. We adjusted and I didn't take on any more jobs. However, I was often consulted on how to go about them. Madge and I had always been fond of making visits to the Ayrshire coast and in the years of Madge's disablement we went more often. We especially liked Troon which was just thirty-five miles from home. It only took about forty-five minutes to get to the sea front, and the front itself was ideal for the wheelchair. We had many wonderful days out at Troon. The people were friendly and we almost felt like residents.

The visit to Buckingham Palace

On New Year's Eve 2003 the telephone rang around midnight. This was normal of course for New Year's and it was our son John. He sounded more than just excited at the celebrations and as he told me his news I relayed it to Madge. He was going to be in the New Year's Honours List. He would receive the CBE which was a Commander of the Most Excellent Order of the British Empire, a grade within the British order of chivalry. It was to be awarded for "services to the development of digital business practices". The ceremony would be held at Buckingham Palace on a date to be scheduled.

    I should have been as excited as any other parent would have been, but having been a doting father all my life, and watching his steady progress, it was not so much a great excitement to me as a great satisfaction that he was about to receive recognition for the work he had put into every project that had come his way. I knew it was a well-earned reward. I was also gratified to discover that not only was John the fourth person from Strathaven to receive a CBE, but all four had come from working class homes. One had a father who was a roadman, one a lorry driver, one a stonemason, and I was a joiner.

    The date for the ceremony at Buckingham Palace was set for the 26th June 2004, and as the day grew closer we made our preparations. However, the number of family and friends allowed to accompany each award winner is naturally restricted and so John's two sons, Mark and Scott, who would have normally been at the Palace, graciously gave up their seats so that Madge and I could enjoy the privilege of seeing their father receive his honour.

    For Madge it was a happy time visiting the shops to see what she would wear. With some help from her daughter-in-law, Elizabeth, the job was done and they found a lovely two-piece suit with a complimentary hat in lavender colour - a very fetching combination. As for me, it was easy because I had recently treated myself to a new suit for any big occasion that might come along. I had bought it shortly before John's news so I was well prepared.

The big day came around and we headed south. We were treated to business class seats on the flight, and a room in a very classy hotel which was a Georgian mansion called the *Cannizaro House* and quite near John's family home in Wimbledon. The weather was wonderful. The ceremony would begin at the Palace at 11am, and the four of us set off in two large taxis with John and his wife Barbara in one, and Madge and me in the other. At the Palace we had to wait a short time to be received into the car park in the Palace grounds, so I got out my camera and began to take snaps through the taxi windows. Later when they were developed I was surprised to see how well they turned out. They seemed quite artistic for a joiner and gave a very good idea of the stately hustle and bustle that goes on at such an event and in such a place.

From the taxis we went into a Reception Area where Madge was taken special care of. She was escorted in her wheelchair by a member of the palace staff to a lift and up to the ballroom, while Barbara and I took another route admiring the grandeur along the way. In the ballroom itself Barbara and I were seated to the right of the platform, in a perfect position to see everything that was about to take place. It was all done in a very relaxed atmosphere. While we enjoyed the atmosphere of the ballroom, and the build-up, and with Madge well-placed in her wheelchair near to the dais, all the actual award recipients, including John, were somewhere else being briefed on the correct procedure to be observed during the ceremony.

On this particular day the awards were to be given out by HRH Prince Charles and before the Prince arrived in the ballroom five members of the Yeomen of the Guard (Queen's Bodyguards) took their places, while the band of the Royal Household Division played. Then the Prince came in with his escort and took his place on the dais as the band went into the National Anthem. After that, everybody settled down and the investitures began. I'm sure that everybody who was there was impressed by the Prince's handling of the proceedings, and the calm but warm way he carried out the traditional task. Nonetheless, it was still heady stuff for us, with a great sense of pride in seeing one of our family honoured by one of the Royal Family.

At the end of the presentations the Prince of Wales departed attended by two orderly officers from the Ghurkhas and we all made our way to meet up again with John. There were some truly wonderful hats on display and Madge had a surprise at photo time to see another lady wearing an absolutely identical hat only a couple of paces away, but for Madge, a woman wearing the same hat at such a grand event was not a cause for concern, it was the stamp of approval saying that she had got it right.

We then made our way out to the Courtyard and I took some more snaps. John's secretary had managed to arrange with the Palace Security for us to go out of the grounds to have our photos taken in front of the main gates and then to get back in. There, outside, we had a surprise because John's two sons were waiting along with their cousins Russell, Kirsty, and Andy, and they all joined us for some family group photographs - the Leggates at Buckingham Palace.

Then we were off to lunch at the Hilton Hotel. It was a big day out and John's reason for the two large taxis to take just four people to the Palace from Wimbledon had become apparent. It was a celebration lunch in a perfect setting with the dining room giving a magnificent view of Buckingham Palace and its grounds. The food was quite superb, and there were many toasts with wine, champagne, and more wine. I think John enjoyed it all more than anyone though none were more proud than Madge and I. I was very glad that Madge was there at Buckingham Palace to experience this honour for the Leggate family because she is no longer with us.

Life in Strathaven

I consider that I have had a very full life and with many highs and a few lows but that's part of life. Mainly, it's gone smoothly. I signed up with the RAF and they gave me a smart uniform, a thorough training, a degree of mechanical knowledge without par, and a sense of application without par. At that time, obviously some of the training had to be condensed and speeded up. That's probably why we did everything at the double, but I'd gone and I'd come back, unlike some of my friends like Wally Charles and others who didn't make it. We got on with life. As I have mentioned, Wally Charles's half-brother was Best Man at our wedding because Wally had been killed.

Even those who didn't actively fight made huge sacrifices and served in the war in their own way. When I was sent to Clydeside the bombs had rained down. In all the big cities people endured a variation of the Blitz. When Madge went off to join the WAAF's her mum and dad had to endure the heavy bombing whilst worrying about their daughter on duty at airfields and RAF establishments because, as they knew, and as everybody now knows, thousands of women in the various services were also killed.

I've had a good social life, particularly through the church, but what I have cherished above most things are the many wonderful friendships that were made as I moved on in my travels through life. For a good number of years after the war ended, those of us who had come home were all very busy getting resettled and adjusted to the changes that were taking place in our lives. Initially there had been a lot of anxiety but by the mid 1950's we had a little more time to spare.

At one point in my life in Strathaven I started to think back to my RAF times and wondered what had become of old colleagues. I realised that I missed them and I asked myself why I'd never made contact with them. I knew that Wally Shaw, an old wartime pal of mine, who had been on our trip to Nassau, lived in a place called Chapelhall about fifteen miles away from my home. He had been a wireless and radar operator on the

Liberators in Nassau. So, one summer when we weren't going away, I decided to try and find Wally. I had never been to Chapelhall but off I went on the bus and I got off in the main street of the town. Then I stood on the pavement wondering where to start. I looked around and began to take things in and I spotted a small grocery shop on the other side of the street.

It was almost as if life had suddenly been slowed down as, like a private detective – the retired military man type of private detective, naturally - I went over to start making my discreet, low key enquiries. There was a young woman behind the counter and I approached her with my questions all ready. However, the case was all but solved in just a few seconds. As I began to tell her about my quest, she politely interrupted and told me that Wally was her cousin, and that, if I hurried back out, I'd catch his brother, who was still across the street at the very same bus stop that she had seen me get off at. I thanked her and as detective life quickened its pace again I went back across the street to make myself known. What a day! I met with my old friend again and in time I became a sort of uncle to his children. They already knew all the old photos of me and Wally and especially the ones of us eating bananas on Paradise Beach.

As we now prepare for this book to be printed, I am told that a researcher is looking up the family of 'Jock' Faulkner, my other old mate from those balmy days of free-time at Paradise Beach. I never knew his real Christian name, only that he came from Gatehouse-of-Fleet, near Edinburgh – a town which seems to be a stronghold of Faulkners. When we were all three out together in the Bahamas – Wally Shaw, 'Jock' and I – we were just three Jocks at Paradise Beach with big smiles on our faces. However, I hear that 'Jock' Faulkner might be from the old Scots family of Faulkner of which the famous American Nobel prize-winning author William Faulkner was also a member. William lived in Oxford, Mississippi and wrote that one of his forebears fought at Culloden and took his claymore and his tartan off to the USA. It's also said that he, William, once visited Gatehouse on his way to Stockholm to collect his award for literature. That his plane from the USA stopped over at Prestwick Airport and he made a quick side-trip to Gatehouse to investigate. We shall see. My son John tells me that a website is going to be set up so that our family and the Leggate story can be updated as we go along. Now, that is truly something.

There are also many other loose ends and stories allied to my own that will appear on the new website - like the whole story of that 'commando raid' (Operation Gauntlet, 1941) up at Spitsbergen in Norway that resulted in a boatload of Norwegian folk ending up in a Scots town while I was employed there in the town building Nissen huts for a camp. The fact that I was building huts was just as well, really. The 'raid' was in fact a big adventure story which needs to be told in its entirety.

As you go along with a book like this one, many facts and coincidences come to light. Like the fact that even when I was starting out as Pony Boy at Dungavel with its little airfield, and the old Duke of Hamilton was still alive, his son Douglas had already purchased some grass meadows and begun work on what would be Glasgow's Prestwick Airport. He would found the airport with his friend David McIntyre, another Scot who had flown with him over Mount Everest, thrilling the world with their exploits.

We are also applying for a 'posthumous' Arctic Star medal which has been struck and issued to commemorate those men like my brother John who served on the Arctic Convoys. There has already been a commemorative service held up at Loch Ewe where many of the convoys sailed from, and a veterans' reunion for those still around. One vet who was 95 years old was initially refused his medal on the basis that he was dead – but he wasn't, and he showed up for the service.

Another one of those coincidences I mentioned is that we used a quote from the author William Faulkner in this book. It's an observation about the past never being dead – the actual quote precedes the family trees section, but we used the quote before realising that 'Jock' might be a relative of his or at least that the Faulkner family came from the same home town.

I can remember all the young men from our own home town, and particularly from the part of town where I'd lived until I was seventeen. I was certain that no other part suffered so many losses in the war. Our home was in the centre of a housing development and I reckon that within a radius of a hundred yards about a dozen men became casualties. Every time I walked or drove around the area, every street, every corner and every building brought back a memory of someone who had once been there and who had died. I'm surrounded by memories of friends and workmates and old YMCA pals who never made it home. Their presence never goes away. Sometimes I feel like the last man standing. Maybe I am that man?

William Bennie Leggate
September 2014

Marjorie's story
written just before she died

Sharing in the making of this book has been a journey for me. I was fascinated as the past unfolded and I studied the records of my ancestors; it brought back so many memories. I wrote to my eldest son, John, who had instigated this book and the historical research: "Thank you, John, for all of the information you sent about my mum and dad. I read it all again this afternoon and was intrigued as I pieced together the jigsaw. I knew Dad's mother bought the shop in Brettenham Road, Edmonton with money that she got when her husband died. I knew he had drowned in the Thames whilst at his work as a Customs officer.

I knew she remarried to Mr William Grimes and he kept the shop going until after WW1. He was a fine gentleman and we used to visit most Sunday nights. The railway ran behind our backdoor at Tottenham and it was just two stops to Angel Road, Edmonton. I liked that outing because I always got a penny bar of chocolate from the machine on the platform. My only remaining cousin is Elsie and she was Aunt Ada's youngest daughter. Aunt Ada was my dad's only sister. She lived until she was 104 and was alert to the very end.

The whole process has brought back many happy memories and I think this is what a family history should do. It should show us our place in the world and who was who. It should link our memories of the past to make more sense of the present. It should also give us a satisfaction and appreciation of who our ancestors were and what they did, what they went through, and what they achieved.

I was a Londoner. I was born at home on the afternoon of 28th October in one of the rooms in a house we rented on a street in Tottenham Hale, in North London. As my mother, who had been born in Hoxton, in the East End of London, never tired of telling everyone, it was a cold Saturday afternoon when she went into labour and my father had *"gone and left her"*. In fact, she was having a little joke, and the truth was rather different: it was a Saturday afternoon and my dad had gone to the football match at nearby White Hart Lane to watch "them Spurs" play. Spurs, of course, are Tottenham Hotspurs Football Club. They're a very famous club and my dad was a Spurs fanatic.

In fact, I was conceived in 1921 during the triumphant season when Spurs won the F.A. Cup for the first time by beating the Wolverhampton Wanderers by one goal to nil. My mum was already carrying me as Spurs knocked out various other teams like Preston and Bradford and Bristol Rovers along their route to the final against the Wolves – (the Wolverhampton Wanderers)

Over the years my dad would tell the story of that year, and especially the 1921 cup final day many times, while mum raised her eyes and went off to make tea. That year, the cup final itself was played at Chelsea in front of nearly 73,000 fans. Chelsea had a better ground but it was April and our traditional April showers had turned into a downpour. The pitch was flooded and the game should have been called off and re-scheduled, but King George had turned up with the Duke of York (the Duke was affectionately known as *Bertie)* - and was introduced to the two teams before the match from under a large umbrella.

Apart from the King, the man-of-the-match was another Bert - Bert Bliss. There were no Wayne's or Rio's in those days and – for what it's worth, no expensive foreign players, either. The Spurs team had two Berts, four Jimmys, a Bob, and a captain called Arthur who didn't join in with the charabanc ride back from Chelsea to Tottenham with the cup but took himself off home to Watford. Afterwards the match report told of "Heavy rain, then some weak sunshine". However, that evening, with most of the team arriving back at Tottenham High Street, the trams were stopped and mounted police struggled to control the crowd which jammed the road. They were Super Spurs that year with four men on the England team that had just played Scotland at Hampden Park, Glasgow, two weeks before the cup final – and where in front of 100,000 fans the Scots had trounced us 3-0.

In fact the *Edmonton Boys* team – Dad came from nearby Edmonton - was basically the "nursery" club for Spurs. I don't know who Dad's beloved team were playing the day I was born, but I like to think that it was the Arsenal who were their deadly rivals from across the other side of North London and nicknamed the Gunners because they had started life at the Royal Arsenal.

In those days watching football was seen as a mostly working class male thing to do although men like the famous classical composer Sir Edward Elgar, and Sir Arthur Conan Doyle (the inventor of Sherlock Holmes) were fanatics, and for what it's worth, Elgar, whose *Pomp and Circumstance March* is played every year at the Proms, supported the Wolves, while Doyle was a founder of the Portsmouth club (Pompey). Going to a home match was a convivial thing to do. There were no seats for the common or garden fans. You stood on the terraces and yelled your heart out although, of course, Dad didn't yell too much because he'd been gassed in the war. It's so sad it's almost comic in a music hall kind of way. The entrance price at the turnstiles was, rather like the players wages at the time, minimal.

My mother's family, including two sisters and a brother, all lived in Tottenham and, as I've said, Dad's family were from nearby Edmonton. Originally, he'd been born in Stepney, within the sound of the Bow Bells, making him a true Cockney, like my mum. Because he'd been gassed in WW1 and badly injured, he had a war pension for life; but it wasn't that much and, like a lot of folk, it was often hard to make ends meet. Dad did his best, but with his health problems he was always going to find it hard to hold down a job. Out of necessity, and while I was still a baby, Mum went back to work as a French polisher at a furniture makers called Harris Lebus, who had a factory nearby on the banks of the river Lea.

Back then, the Lea Valley was still a lovely rural place, with cottages, cottage gardens and apple orchards, but change was in the air as it gradually grew into a bustling industrial hub. You could still walk along the river and imagine you were in the countryside, even though factories were expanding along the canal and along the developing railways. The timber used for the furniture-making used to come down the River Lea on barges. I had a friend whose uncle worked on the barges and if he was working we would go down there and watch. We thought it was great.

Harris Lebus were the biggest furniture makers in the world. They had such a sprawling site over many acres that they even had an entire railway spur and yards built to cater for their expanding trade and their comings and goings. This proved very useful later on in WW2 when the company switched from making furniture to making planes. There was even an airfield in Norfolk filled with dummy planes made of wood by Lebus that was designed to fool the Germans into thinking we had more planes than we actually had. They also made Sherman tanks out of wood which were also designed to fool the enemy. It was not a new idea. Back in WW1, there had also been wooden models called Timber Tommies which were groups of wooden models giving the impression that infantry had already clambered up and over the top of the trenches and were about to attack across "no man's land". Anything to cause doubt and confusion in the enemy's mind, I suppose, and I always wondered if Harris Lebus had made them, too, but that's really just another sad thought.

When I was six we moved into the house next door to our rented home in Tottenham, where we had a lot more space. This was also rented but to my delight, I had an entire room to myself. There was a shortage of houses in the thirties, but when I was eight or nine mum and dad managed to buy one about five miles away at a place called Enfield Wash. The house was terraced, but new and it cost about £450. The mortgage repayments turned out to be about half of what mum and dad had been paying before in rent, so financially, we were much better off. In addition we now had electricity, a bathroom and, as if that wasn't enough, there was a garden back and front. It was bliss. Dad thought he was in clover because he loved to garden and previously, he only had an allotment, where he grew vegetables. Allotments are now considered chic, but in our new garden Dad could grow vegetables as well as flowers. He loved his carnations, which always made a fine display.

Life continued to get better. I was a bright girl, although I do say it myself, and at age eleven, after primary school, I won a scholarship to Tottenham High School for Girls, and I travelled there by tram each day for six years. It was a private school, originally built for the children of the Drapers Guild, one of the traditional old clothing trade guilds of London. I received a very good education at Tottenham High School and I had just completed my school leaving exam in 1939, and was about to start a sixth year course in business studies, when war broke out. The school was evacuated to the Essex countryside and I went with it, returning home in the summer of 1940.

My school days were over and I got an office job. I started work in the accounts department at the Cosmos lamp and chemical works in Brimsdown, Enfield that August. Despite their posh name, at the time they only made electric light bulbs, but with war that changed and they were soon making radar equipment. I don't think my life would have been very different had the war not interrupted it. Very few working class people in my younger days went on to university, so I would have left, got the office job that I got, and then married someone local.

I have little doubt that I would have remained in London, but the war changed a lot of things for many people, and it certainly moved my life in an entirely unexpected direction. I kept a very detailed diary for 1940, another for 1941, and later in this book you can see a few extracts. I hope you will take into consideration that I was not a war correspondent but a schoolgirl.

As I have said, I was evacuated with my school to the countryside of Saffron Walden in Essex, away from the bombs falling on London to the end of 1941, and then I got a job. I joined the WAAFs in 1942.

I have re-read the diaries and all I can say is that it is what it is. Just about every page is packed with, mostly, what's happening in the war and to a lesser extent some of the things in my personal life. A young girl is exactly that – a young girl. The events and my comments had just tumbled onto the pages and were formed from all various influences in my life.

Friday 24 May 1940

The King gave a very fine speech tonight which was broadcast throughout the Empire, also to the USA, where it made a very good impression, for the Americans are still deciding whether to enter this war or not. Fierce fighting in France. Boulogne captured by the Germans. Arras gap 25 miles wide through which Germans are passing. German pressure still south of Paris. French and Germans are bombing border towns. RAF still bombing German places of communication in Germany. 80 German planes down since yesterday. 500 lost this week, told of 1500 since 10 May. The position is still very serious. More people being arrested on suspicion. Refugees still pouring into England. RAF is doing magnificent work and the men are daring and full of courage.

Went for a walk this afternoon with Amy and Jean and we found a sheltered grass bank where we had a glorious rest and read. It made a pleasant change.

Today is a National Day of Prayer, as decreed by the King, and the churches and chapels all over the Empire have been packed to overflowing. I have been to the parish church this morning and evening. Lovely parcel from home, containing plenty of things to eat.

Thursday 13 June

The Germans have almost reached Paris now, for they are but 15 miles away. Paris has been declared an open city to save it from destruction from air raids. We are sending thousands of men to France and also those *withdrawn from Norway. The position is so serious that the French Prime Minister has asked for America's help, but they will only send munitions, guns, but will not enter the war.*

This evening Amy and Jessie came to tea and supper and we had quite a good time all together and they thoroughly enjoyed themselves. Letter from home.

Friday 14 June
PARIS HAS FALLEN.

Monday 22 June
Well this afternoon I left school and I must say it was with some regret because I really have had a very happy school life and have made some good friends.

After I started my job at the Cosmos works, I continued with my diary throughout 1941 until I joined the WAAFs in 1942. I described how the war was taken to Germany, North Africa, mainland Europe, from Italy and the Balkans to Scandinavia and the Russian Front. I conjured up exotic names in the Far East, where battles are fought against Japan, while anguishing over why America wouldn't join in until Pearl Harbour was attacked at the end of 1941. I also described small details of books I read, films I saw and clothes I made from material bought in London's street markets, demonstrating how in the midst of earth-shattering big events, people somehow managed to go about their everyday lives.

Monday 3 February 1941

Well, just because we are to go on Fire Watch duty tonight a heavy fall of snow has come down, just our luck, but perhaps it will keep them away. Mum and I sat in the draughty little hut or garden shed surrounded by a small oil stove which perfumed the air with Ashes of Paraffin, a lamp, rickety chair and a dratted alarm clock with a deadly tick. It nearly drove me frantic. When the raid was in progress we sat with tin helmets on and looked generally mad. We were glad when it was time to knock up the next two watchers, but it is a vital service.

Saturday 22 February

Last night was noisy again but I slept upstairs. I bought a new hat this afternoon, a tiny maroon affair but quite pretty. I saw two very good films at the Savoy, "I Love You Again", a comedy starring Myrna Loy and William Powell, and a very clever thriller, "The Secret Seven".

Thursday 20 March

Worst raid we have ever had on London last night. Fires seem to spring up from nowhere. The guns were firing without ceasing, flares were dropped in their hundreds and of course H. E. incendiaries and land mines were far too numerous. Edmonton, Ponders End and the dock areas, the City – well all of London – was severely affected .The Battle of the Atlantic is raging fiercely too; we are losing far too many ships full of important cargoes, food and material. Meat ration cut to 11d this week, rest is corned beef. Edmonton was very badly damaged by landmines and bombs and a heavy casualty list is suspected. Plymouth was badly raided last night though here it was very quiet, but strangely enough though I slept through the worst on Wednesday. Last night, I just couldn't sleep. Position in Yugoslavia is very strange, the people do not want Hitler but the government does.

Saturday 22 March

This afternoon I bought some very pretty material, it is very pretty indeed and quite reasonable, only 2/6 ¾ (two shillings, sixpence and three farthings) a yard. I saw "Mark of Zorro" with Tyrone Power and Linda Darnell. It was excellent.

Friday 4 April

Tonight news has come thro' that Teleeki, the Hungarian Prime Minister, has shot himself dead and his wife is seriously ill. What a tragedy! We have lost Benghazi, the Libyan port, to German and Italian troops, but we have something up our sleeves, I am sure! Well, more rain. Today I am going to St George's for a club dance and then I must go on Fire Watch from 10 – 12. What a life!

Thursday 26 June

I do feel despondent tonight and the sole reason is that I have been reading a book "Blood Relations" by P. Gibbs about 1914-1918 , of an

English girl who marries a German count just before the outbreak of the war. There are some vivid descriptions but it has made me very thoughtful. Good rationing news, we are to have 2lbs extra sugar per book for jam and we may get 6d more meat allowance.

Friday 27 June

The weather seems to be breaking, and still I trip to work without coat or stockings. The Germans are breaking thro' the Russian lines at several points but they are having severe losses too. The RAF again heavily bombed N. France during daylight. Good work all round really. Sweden has stated she is willing to let German troops thro' her territory, what a blow that must be for Finland. Sweden refused when we wanted to help them. What a strange world we are living in.

Thursday 24 July

The Battle of Russia is really and truly a modern war with all the terrible atrocities; villages are being plundered, innocent people murdered and millions of soldiers are facing one another, but for what is all this blood being shed? Will we reach our goal? We must, it is our duty, every one of us to fight on to the bitter end.

Tonight the air is baking, it is like the heat wave again, but no doubt a storm will break before long! Just our luck!

Monday 1 September

Well, September 1st dawned in the time old manner, a thick mist but a shining sun. Today is supposedly invasion day but nothing has happened up to yet, though last night our guns stretched themselves and made rather a row.

Tuesday 2 September

Well, as Connie is away on holiday I have had plenty to do at work. I wish Miss White wouldn't talk so much. She nearly drove me scatty today. Poor Iris has to do all the work whilst she stands gassing.

Tuesday 28 October

Well, today I reached the ripe old age of 19. I have done very well, considering this wretched war. 30/- in money, bolero, nice fountain pen, 5/- book token, stockings and also a pair of shoes promised from Mum with the coupons too. It is freezing cold and I have hugged the fire all the evening.

Thursday 13 November

The American Neutrality Club is missed by only a very narrow margin. The USA people are definitely not even 60% behind us, yet we are fighting for them as well. They seem to be interested in the money problems. The weather this week is simply putrid. It has rained every day and has been freezing cold.

Friday 14 November

A sad blow today: The Ark Royal has sunk in the Mediterranean. She was torpedoed and whilst being towed was sunk. How can Germany announce her loss, for according to them she has sunk at least six times before? Though there were 1600 men on board only 18 are missing, which is a great comfort for everyone.

Monday 17 November

Millions of our women are needed immediately in ammunitions works but unfortunately, they seem to be very slow in coming forward. I shouldn't really shout as what am I doing? NOTHING! I had a letter and a hankie from Dorothy. I was surprised. Americans captured German boat near S. America. It was flying American colours etc. but their plans failed.

Friday 28 November

A bill is being passed compelling everyone between 18 and 50 to do direct war work. The women up to 30 will be put in the forces and the others in factories. It probably means that I shall have to join up but I shan't really mind.

Sunday 7 December

Roosevelt announced tonight that Japanese planes have attacked the American bases in Hawaii. Big Libyan battle. Everyone thinks that the Germans are beaten but I doubt it somehow.

Monday 8 December

Japan has declared war on Britain and USA!

Throughout the rest of December I described how Germany and Italy declared war on the USA and how almost the entire world was at war. I wrote that *"It's a terrible state of affairs."*

N.B. My diary concluded on New Year's Eve, 1941, where I described how I went to a New Year's dance. Sadly, life was so full, first with the war and then with marriage and children, that I wasn't able to return to keeping a diary until the 1950s, after which I kept up a simple appointments diary for many years.

In 1942 my orders had arrived in the post. I had to sign up for some kind of war service - either factory work, or in one of the armed forces. So I joined the WAAFs, the Women's Auxiliary Air Force. For a year I was stationed at Number One Balloon Centre at Kidbrooke, near Eltham, in South London, working in the accounts department. It was there that I met Doris. She's been a lifelong friend since then, who now lives in Llandudno in North Wales, and we still correspond. Most people in the services were sent anywhere they needed a body to fill a gap, but I was lucky. After Kidbrooke, I was sent to St Athan in South Wales, to the massive RAF airfield there, and I stayed put for the duration.

I met Bill at a dance in a local village hall in the March of 1944. We got engaged in the August of that year and married the following April, about a month before the war ended in Europe. Bill had been posted to the West Indies in 1944/5 and on the way back from there, via the USA and Canada, he bought me some lovely accessories to go with a wedding dress that had been loaned to me by a WAAF friend of mine. Bill also bought me a suit, shoes and matching gloves as a going away outfit. I would never have been able to get any of those things in Britain because clothing was on ration and my ration allowance would barely have outfitted a flea. I didn't have enough clothing coupons to buy my own wedding dress and that's why a friend lent me one, but I didn't care. I was so happy.

I was demobbed in November 1945 and Bill was demobbed in the December which was early for a serviceman but it was because he was in the building trade and houses were once again in short supply and his services were needed urgently. Quite where they got that "urgently" bit from I don't know. Maybe it was an assessment of the average number of builders required for the whole country, or maybe it was someone from the Ministry of Optimism, because Bill found it hard to get work and had to really persevere.

At times it felt like I had come full circle; from the housing shortage when I was born after WW1, and then to another after WW2, but now I had Bill. We were also very optimistic and looked forward to the future. I arrived in Strathaven on Christmas Eve and there I was, waiting for Christmas to happen, as it had always happened in London. However, and it took me a while, eventually I realised that nobody up here in Strathaven was going to do Christmas. There wasn't going to be much celebrating. Even Santa's services were not needed urgently. Christmas Day dawned just like another normal working day in Strathaven where the shops were all open and there was mince and tatties and gravy for dinner.

Six thousand souls in the town and they were all waiting for the New Year which was what the Scots celebrated instead of Christmas. It would be many years before people stopped working on Christmas Day in Scotland. The upside was that the New Year celebrations were great fun with lots of singing and dancing, and the English didn't celebrate New Year like the Scots. Back then, and in many ways, Scotland was another country altogether, with a completely different way of life, or so it seemed.

We had moved in with Bill's family. The house was a corporation house with four bedrooms. It was quite a big house, really, compared with many, but there were a lot of us. Bill had six brothers and two sisters, all living at home, except for Bill's brother John, who was a regular navy man and was still away serving. His absence didn't make for a spare space though, because a friend of Bill's dad was also in residence. Apart from the war years, I'd gone from being a single child with her own room, an indoor toilet and bathroom in London, to being jammed up within a small room with my new husband and sharing everything with a very big family. The food was different, too, and although it was more plentiful than in London, it was not as varied. Mince was the traditional number one food here. The main vegetables were the aforementioned "tatties", which were potatoes, and carrots, and the turnips which were called "neeps". Fruit was not exactly high on the agenda, either. Feeding a lot of people on Bill's dad's postman's wage meant buying enough of the kind of food that fills you up and not buying exotic stuff.

At first, it was a bit of a culture shock. Despite having been away from home during the war, I'd been with a group of other girls around my age. Life in the WAAFs for us was like going away to boarding school – or what I'd read in books that life at boarding schools was like - and, even though it was wartime, we girls had fun and I made many friends. However, I was young and newly married and very happy with Bill, so I was determined to do my best to fit into life in this strange land.

Despite my good intentions, for some never explained reason there was a lot of hostility directed at me immediately. I felt like the war bride who was captured by a raiding party and then dragged back behind Hadrian's Wall. Except I wasn't treated like a slave I was treated like I shouldn't be there. With Bill straight away off out looking for work and then finding work, I felt lonely, lost and confused and was soon wondering day in and day out what on earth I'd got myself into. Perhaps I was naïve to think I could just fit in and take my place in a very crowded household ruled over by a strong matriarchal figure. Obviously I hadn't been brought up to understand the "Scottish Manner". Now it couldn't have been easy for Mrs Leggate to suddenly have this English daughter-in-law staying with her. Perhaps because I came from London she felt that I was more worldly and had some kind of cosmopolitan air. I never even considered the possibility that perhaps she would have preferred a good Scottish wife for her son.

Grandpa Leggate was very kind to me. The three younger boys were almost a second family. My Bill had been twenty one when his youngest brother was born. I suddenly became quite handy as a nursemaid and helped with another young brother called Richard who was handicapped and had difficulty speaking. Poor Richard and I took to one another immediately. I could understand him more than his mother could at times. In fact, Mrs Leggate often used to swallow her pride and ask me to translate and to tell her what the boy was trying to say.

In order to get out of the house and be able to think straight and try to work out what I was doing wrong - if I was doing anything wrong at all - I'd take Richard on long walks all around the district and into the countryside. Without realising it, I was retracing many of the walks that

Bill took as a boy with his grandfather and I was soaking up its quiet beauty. I continued to try to help around the house without getting under Mrs Leggate's feet. She wouldn't let me help much with anything. I would have liked a proper job away from the house that I could go to every day, but back then and especially in Scotland women didn't really work, except in some shops, and there was nothing available for me.

In 1947 Bill and I had a son whom we named John which meant there were three Johns in the house - and four when Bill's elder brother was home on leave from the navy. However, and as Bill has no doubt written, that summer Bill's parents gave up their council house tenancy and bought a house in North Street, helped in part with money that Bill and I provided from our war service annuity. We moved with them but it still didn't work. Bill and I were moving apart from them. It had never been a happy relationship. Getting a council house seemed a local option. I was quite surprised. Oh, God. Down south I had never even been inside one. Down south council houses were only for poor people. However, in Scotland all kinds of middle-class professionals and lawyers and teachers also wanted to get one. It was like someone once told me later about Welsh country people who bought proper baked bread until the new sliced bread arrived, and then bought the sliced not because it was better but because it was considered a step up.

So the idea was that you got on the council housing list and you waited until you got one. In Strathaven at that time there were also a lot of dwellings nicknamed "single ends". These were simple one roomed houses but after living in the crowded Leggate household, I would have loved to have had one. It seemed that with so many people returning from the war, and with the bombing that Glasgow took, council housing anywhere, and housing in general, was in very short supply. After finding out the council waiting list was about seven years long Bill managed to pull a few strings and, in a very short space of time, bought a low-cost house in North Street - just along the road from his parents.

At times this proximity proved awkward, given the cool relationship that now existed between us. North Street is one of Strathaven's oldest streets with the castle nearby. At one time the street was called Pipers Row because it was where a lot of the castle's workers lived. We moved into the house in 1948, three years after our wedding. I was over the moon to get a place of our own. It was a three story building, known as a tenement house, with plenty of room in which to expand as the years passed.

To start with, we had four tenants in the house. They each had a room and a kitchen except for one tenant who was happy with just an attic room. We allowed ourselves the other attic, with an extra room for a bit more space and a kitchen. I was overjoyed to be finally able to cook our own meals. My mother, who had been a wonderful cook, had trained me well, and I was soon experimenting with my own recipes. I became an enthusiastic baker and made all our own bread.

The plan was to live simply and pay back our house loan as quickly as possible. With me managing the home together with Bill's hard work, this was achieved within six months - something that would be impossible for anyone now without inheriting money, or doing something like winning the lottery. We never had a mortgage. We've had two houses since North Street and we've paid them off straight away. For many years the house was busy with young families and their children and our boys and all kinds of different school friends all coming and going. Of course we were busy adding to our own family. John was twelve when our youngest, Andrew, was born. As we went along I made it my job to make sure they all stuck to their books and studied hard. Like all children they were sometimes argumentative, but all of them have done well and made good marriages. To me a happy marriage is a very big thing in life.

Gradually, as our tenants moved out to houses of their own, and with Bill's expertise as a joiner and all-round builder, we converted the house to a single family dwelling. It was no longer a tenement, but a beautiful townhouse, and it was always a happy house. I became more and more like one of the Strathaven folk, integrating until I was one of them. In the nicest way, and with all respect, I fell in love again: with Strathaven; a sleepy wee market town of six thousand inhabitants.

I joined a Women's Rural, (a Rural Committee). I was a hospital visitor for some thirty five years (I had to stop after my accident). From the start of my life in Strathaven I attended a church where I did a lot of social work and made plenty of friends. I recall a time when a lot of new houses were built in the new town of East Kilbride, some seven or eight miles from Strathaven. There was an influx of English folk because the building managers were sent up from England with their families to oversee and set up the construction. I was with a whole group of women, English and Scots, and we were talking about various things and I said, "Now, remember that I'm English," and one of the Scots women said: "Oh, away with ye! Ye're one of us."

I thought that was one of the nicest things. It made me realise that I'd settled in. Strathaven is a lovely wee place. The years passed and after all our own sons had grown and left home, and with their own lives to manage, we converted the bottom two rooms and kitchen into one self-contained flat for my own mum and dad who by then needed some help. They moved up to Scotland in 1972 and lived with us for the next six years.

In 1985 our son David bought the North Street house from us and Bill and I moved to a nearby village called Chapelton, before moving back again six years later to Strathaven to our present house near the park. In 1997 I had the accident – which Bill has written about so I won't go over it again.

I'd always been very active. I had been quite a gardener through all my married life, growing vegetables for the table, and I also had a knitting machine, but as well as broken legs I had a badly dislocated shoulder and had to give up those activities. I was in the hospital for three months and then had bone grafts, but when I contracted MRSA the doctors said that with my immune system down, they couldn't do any more grafts because I would not recover from an operation. I was in plaster for three years, but with lots of love and help both on the medical side and from friends, I got back on my feet and was able to move around a bit.

I even recovered sufficiently enough to take holidays abroad. Then, fifteen years on from the accident, which wasn't bad considering my age and condition combined, I finally had to get an electric wheelchair. Having been so active in the past I find it all frustrating. I know that I won't walk again and I just have to accept it. At the moment I still prepare meals and do the washing and the ironing from my wheelchair, but I don't shop anymore which I miss. In compensation we get a lot of visitors and hardly a day goes by without someone dropping by for tea and a chat. These days, it's mainly our old friends' children because all the old friends have departed.

Marjorie Constance Leggate - 2013

Leggate Family Tree

William Faulkner - the Nobel prize-winning American author from Mississippi – once observed that: "The past is never dead. It's not even the past."

The genealogist Anthony Adolph says that we modern day Scottish Leggates (two g's) are probably descended from an Adam Legate of the 13th century whose job was to be a legate and to collect taxes. A legate was his job description. Just like someone could be called Adam Footballer – in fact there was once a footballer called Archie Leggate who was very famous and played for Scotland. At one time he scored the fastest hat trick ever (3 goals in one match) - albeit for Fulham. Archie also went to live in Canada along with many Scots.

**To see the full family history please visit
www.leggatefamily.com**

Bill's Family Tree 1

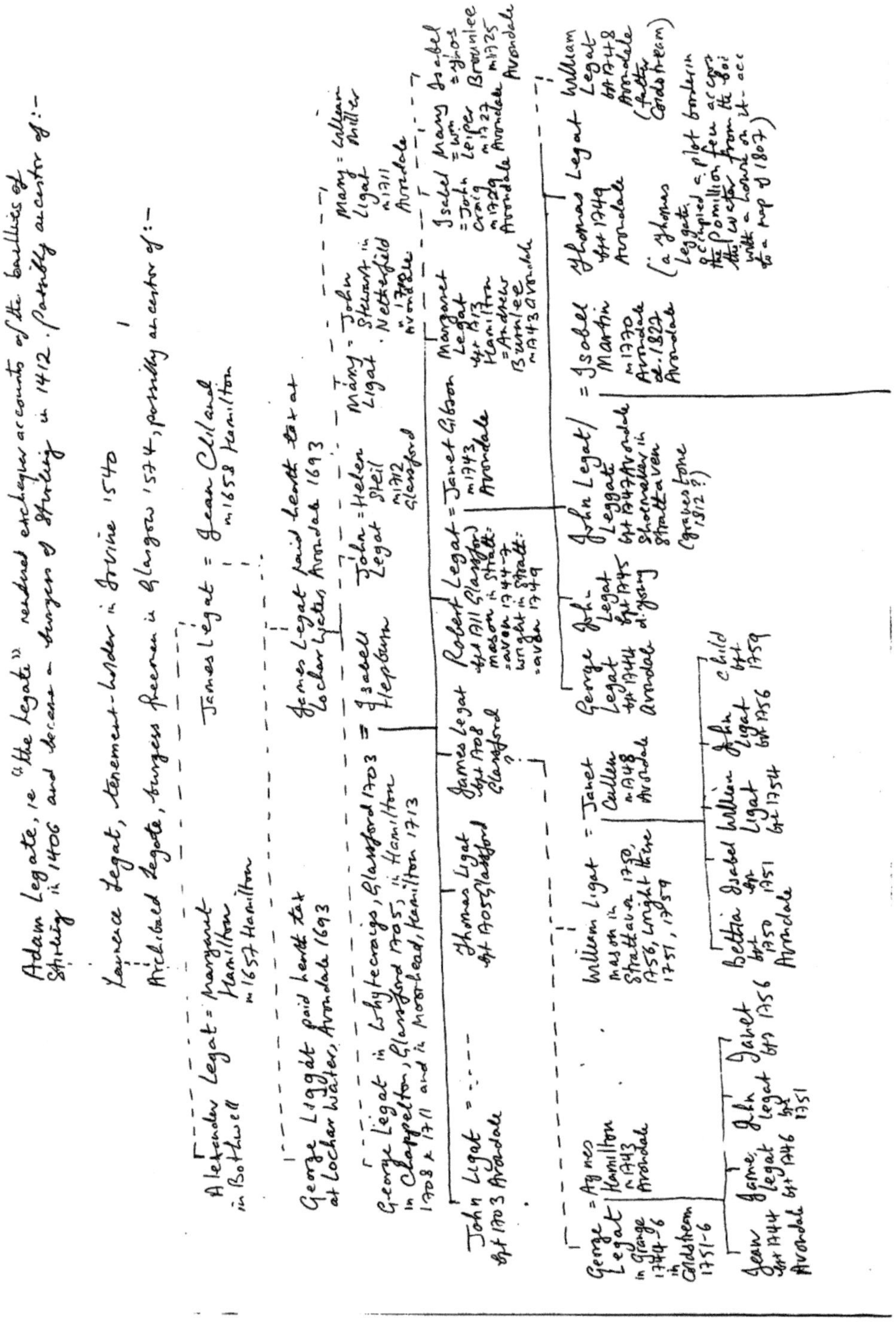

[Handwritten family tree, rotated 90°. Transcription of contents below:]

Adam Legate, re "the Legate" received exchequer accounts of the bailliries of Stirling in 1406 and became burgess of Stirling in 1412. Possibly ancestor of :—

Laurence Legat, tenement-holder in Irvine 1540
Archibald Legate, burgess freeman in Glasgow 1574, possibly ancestor of :—

James Legat = Jean Cleland
m 1658 Hamilton

James Legat paid hearth tax at Lochwinnoch, Avondale 1693

Alexander Legat = Margaret Hamilton, m 1657 Hamilton, in Bothwell

George Liggat paid hearth tax at Lochar Water, Avondale 1693

George Legat in Libytecraigs, Blanford 1703 = Isabell Hepburn
George Legat in Clappelton, Blanford mas, in Hamilton 1708 & 1711 and in Moorhead, Hamilton 1713

John Ligat b. 1703 Avondale

Thomas Ligat bpt 1708 Glanford

James Legat bpt 1708 Glanford

Robert Legat = Janet Gibson
bpt 1711 (Planton) m 1743, Avondale
mason in Strath: avon 1744-7
Ligat in Strath: avon 1749

John Legat = Helen Sheil
Legat m 1712 Glanford
John Shrump in Nettlefield 1719 Avondale

Mary Ligat

Mary = William Miller
Ligat m 1711 Avondale

Isabel Mary Isabel
= John = Wm = Jnot
Craig Lesper Brownlee
m 1729 m 27 m 1725
Avondale Avondale Avondale

William Ligat mason in Strathavon 1730, A56, Wright there 1751, 1759

Bettia Ligat bpt 1752

Isobel Ligat bpt 1751

William Ligat bpt 1754

John Ligat bpt 1756

child bpt 1759

= Janet Cullen m 1748 Avondale

George John Legat bpt 1744 Avondale d. young

John Legat bpt 1747 Avondale shoemaker in Strathaven (Gravestone 1812?)

Margaret Legat bpt 1713 = Andrew Hamilton-Brownlee m 1743 Avondale

= Isobel Martin m 1770 Avondale d. 1822 Avondale

Thomas Legat bpt 1749 Avondale

William Legat bpt 1748 Avondale (later Coldstream)

(a Thomas Legat occupied a plot bordering the Pomillon feu at Lygs, with a house on it — acc to a map of 1807)

George Legat = Agnes Hamilton m 1743 Avondale, in Grange 1744-6 in Coldstream 1751-6

Jean bpt 1744 Avondale

James Legat bpt 1746

Janet Legat bpt 1751

Bill's Family Tree 2

Marjorie's Family Tree 1

Henry James Burn(s) =
glazier

[Henry Burn was described on son's marriage certificate as "father Henry Burns, jockey", deceased]

Thomas Grady slater dead by 1894

Henry Burn
b c.1831 London
coachman/groom
of Harriett Sq, Stonehill
in 1891
dead by 1891

= (1 Ellen Fitzgerald 2) = Callaghan b. by 1894
b c.1865/6

m. 1) ---
m. 2) 18/6/1894
St Anne's, Old St
witnesses Alfred Selwood
Winter & Emily Regina Williams

Henry Alfred or A(lfre)
Henry Burn(s)
b " London "
or " Kent "
European artist maker/
sculpture maker
of Westmoreland Place

Alice Burns
b 1888

Katie Burns
b 1891

Ellen Burns
b 1900(?)

Robert Jones
ag. lab. of
Hotfield, Kent

= Mary
b c.1791 Boughton
(under Blean?) Kent

= Sophia Jones
b c.1834 Hotfield, Kent
m. 28/7/1856 St Matthew
Bethnal Green, witness
William & Amy Porter

George Jones
b c.1836 Hotfield, Kent

9632 Jones
b 1830
Hotfield

Esther M.
b 1859/9
St John's
Hackney
seamstress

Thomas Burn
b 1863
Hotfield

George Burn
b 1866
Hotfield

John Burn
b 1869
Stonehill
Shoemaker

Sophia ("Georgie")
Burns
b 6 August 1897
Westmoreland Pla. Stonehill

= Stephen Knight

↓

Marjory Constance Knight

Anthony Adolph May 2013

Marjorie's Family Tree 2

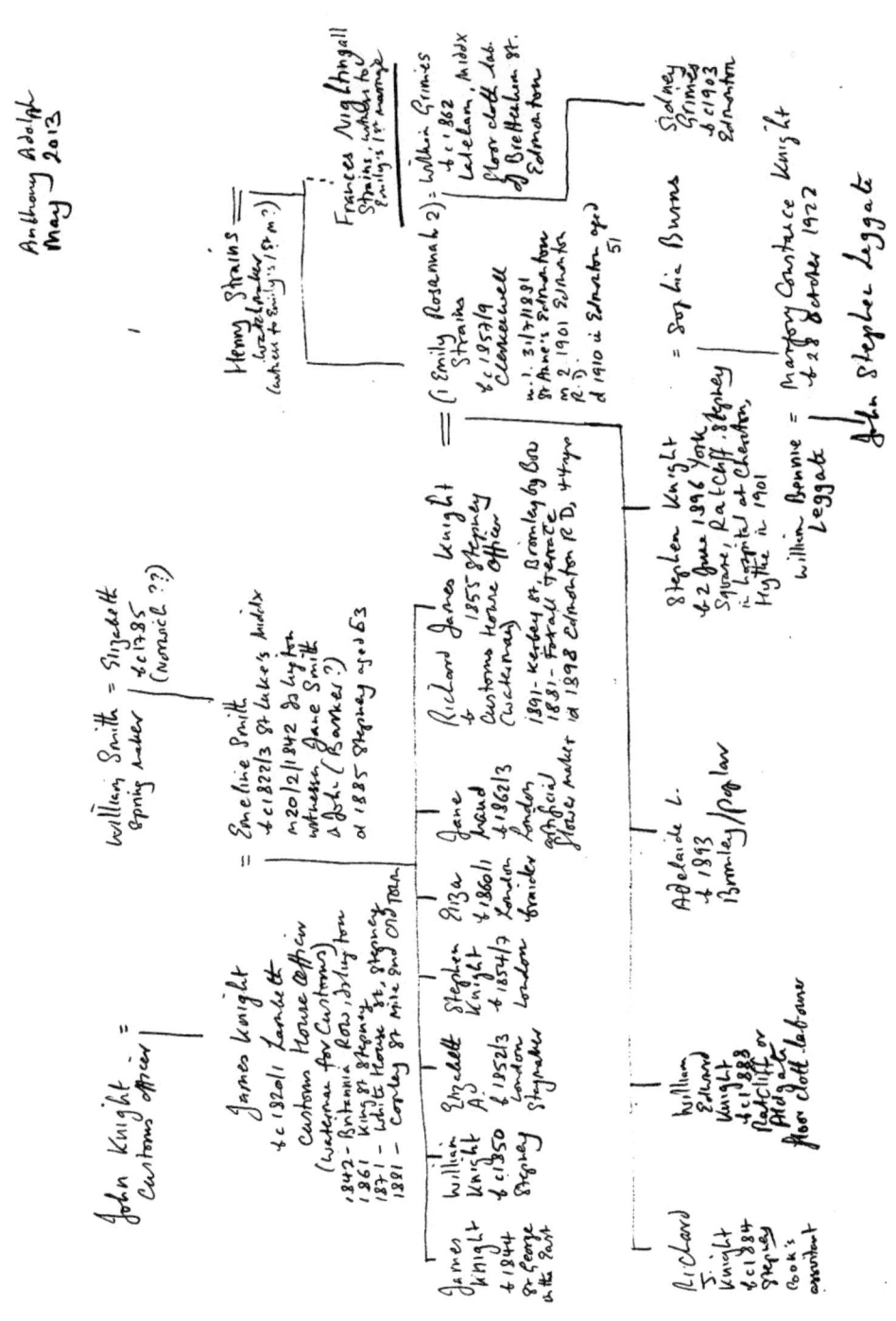

The Crown and its links with the Dukes of Hamilton
A note from Strathaven historian Robert Currie

N.B. We would like to express sincere thanks to Bob Currie for the use in this book of some of his collection of old photographs. Bob very kindly allowed the use of the photos at no cost. He was also very generous with his knowledge of local affairs, and, indeed, Scottish affairs. This is what he wrote:

I feel privileged in contributing what, in essence, is a small piece to this memoir of Bill Leggate. I often called on Bill's late mother at her home in North Street, Strathaven as an elder and member of the Kirk Session of Avendale Old Parish Church. On those many pastoral visits she shared her memories of Strathaven's past with me. From past to present now makes an astonishing leap, since I never imagined that in the space of forty plus years I should become a contributor to this work on the life and times of Mrs. Leggate's son who is now aged 92. That said, I thank Bill for the honour of contributing, and I have cobbled these few paragraphs together on the Ducal family, it's associations with the Honours of Scotland, those of the United Kingdom and, not least, Strathaven itself.

Within the pages of this book the reader will have already learned how, as a teenager, Bill Leggate served as a Pony Boy to the Duke of Hamilton on his country estate of Dungavel, near Strathaven. At that period in time Dungavel, set within a Grouse Moor, was the Duke's Hunting Lodge. However, his main residence had been the imposing Hamilton Palace (modelled on the more famous Buckingham Palace) with its truly magnificent Petit Palace of Chatelherault, a name derived from the French town of that name, the title of Duc de Chatelherault also being held by the Duke of Hamilton.

Dungavel – this former hunting lodge of the now demolished Hamilton Palace - was designed by William Adam and completed in 1734. It comprises two pavilions linked by a gateway. The north facade was visible from the palace and forms the front of the building. To the rear are the formal parterre gardens. The buildings provided kennels, stables and accommodation for hunting parties returning from the woodlands to the south. Adam jokingly referred to his creation as "The Dog Kennel". An avenue of lime trees linked the lodge and the palace formerly located in

Hamilton. When absent from these locally based residencies the Duke enjoyed life at his house in London.

Strathaven's historic links with the Hamilton's stretch back to 1643 when the Ducal family of Hamilton – a title in the Peerage of Scotland was created. Hamilton is the senior dukedom in that Peerage (except for the Dukedom of Rothesay which is held by the Sovereign's eldest son), and as such its holder is the Premier Peer of Scotland as well as being head of both the House of Hamilton and the House of Douglas. The Ducal surname, originally "Hamilton" is now "Douglas Hamilton". Since 1711, the Dukedom has been held together with the Dukedom of Brandon in the Peerage of Great Britain and the Dukes since that time have been styled Duke of Hamilton and Brandon.

In the absence of a resident Scottish monarch following the Union of the Crowns in 1603, when James VI of Scotland inherited the throne of England and moved his Royal Household from Edinburgh to London, the Honours were carried to sittings of the Parliament of Scotland to symbolise the sovereign's presence and the Royal Assent.

On 24th June 1953, following her coronation at Westminster Abbey, in London, the Scottish crown was carried before Her Majesty Queen Elizabeth in a procession from the Palace of Holyrood house to the High Kirk of St Giles, Edinburgh, where the Honours of Scotland, including the crown, were presented to the Queen during a National Service of Thanksgiving.

More recently, the crown has been presented at the Official Opening ceremonies of sessions of the Scottish Parliament, including the first meeting of the modern Parliament in 1999 and the official opening of the new Scottish Parliament Building in 2004. On such occasions the crown, carried by Scotland's Premier Duke of Hamilton, the hereditary bearer of the crown of Scotland, immediately precedes Her Majesty the Queen in the custom of the ancient ceremonial procession known as the Riding of Parliament.

Currently, Scotland faces an uncertain political future as she wrestles with the question of independence. This will soon be decided by a Referendum when its people will vote on whether to remain within the framework of the United Kingdom, or to declare in favour of an independent country. Significantly, amidst all the uncertainty, the architects of the Referendum – the Scottish National Party (SNP) has pledged to maintain Scotland's historic links with the British Crown. The Scottish Government's proposal is that the Queen remains Head of State in Scotland in the same way as she is Head of State in independent countries such as Canada, Australia and New Zealand. This pledge is encapsulated in the words of a latter day Poet Laureate and was penned to mark the occasion of Queen Elizabeth's marriage to Prince Philip, Duke of Edinburgh, in 1947.

To those dear lands, still calling Britain "Home"
The Crown is still the link with Britain's past
The consecrated thing that must outlast
Folly and hate and other human foam.

There is a significant irony that in the event of Scotland gaining independence, Queen Elizabeth the Second and her successors would remain as Head of State in Scotland and the Duke of Hamilton and his heirs would continue as hereditary bearers of the Crown of Scotland, immediately preceding Her Majesty the Queen and/or her successors in the custom of the ancient opening ceremonial procession of the "Riding of Parliament".

All of that will depend on whether or not an independent Scotland chooses to continue as a monarchy in the referendum on 18th September.

Bob Currie. Strathaven - 2014

List of illustrations

Cover – Bill and two mates at Paradise Beach

Back – Boo Backit Brig over the Pomilion, Strathaven
Strathaven in Old Picture Postcards, Bob Currie,
European Library, 1988

1. Madge and Bill - RAF
2. Dungavel House back then
3. Dungavel House today
4. Strathaven
5. Strathaven volunteers
6. Strathaven station
7. Strathaven railway staff
8. Strathaven postal workers
9. The Duke of Hamilton
10. Harry Lauder
11. Harry Lauder long-playing record
12. John Leggate on horseback
13. Young Madge
14. Young Madge
15. Young Madge
16. Grandma Burns
17. Madge's mother
18. Madge's parents
19. Uncle Mick Burns
20. John Leggate
21. Arctic Star medal
22. Two of Bill's crew mates
23. Bill aged 19
24. Bill hitting the bull's eye
25. RAF Gunnery School
26. The New Amsterdam
27. Bill, Jock and Wally Shaw
28. Bill, Jock and Wally in summer kit
29. Liberator crew
30. Diving platform (2)
31. RAF boxing team
32. Wally Charles
33. Bill playacting
34. The Duchess of Windsor
35. Wedding picture
36. Wedding picture
37. Madge with baby John
38. Leggate family
39. Leggate children
40. Madge – New York
41. At Buckingham Palace
42. Diary cover -1940
43. Postcard
44. Postcard
45. Italo Balbo
46. Map of GB
47. Map of USA east coast

More photos at www.leggatefamily.com

1. Wallet shots of Madge and me just before we met

2. Dungavel House

3. Dungavel Centre

4.

Strathaven Volunteers photographed in the last decade of the nineteenth century.
Front row: first, second and third left respectively: Mr. Leggate, Mr. Owens & Sergeant Kennedy.
The volunteers trained on Primrose Braes. Sergeant Kennedy was Janitor and Drill Sergeant at Strathaven Academy.
He subsequently drilled Strathaven's First World War recruits before they left for their military postings.

5.

Strathaven Central Station.

6.

Employees of Caledonian Railway - Strathaven North Station
This picture pre-dates The First World War.

7.

Strathaven postal workers and officials on the occasion of the presentation of Long Service Medals to Mr. John Leggate and Mr. Colin Sommerville

8.

His Grace Alfred Douglas, 13th Duke of Hamilton and
10th Duke of Brandon.
(1911)

9.

Sir Harry Lauder

Born   4 August 1870
              Portobello, Edinburgh, Scotland, UK

Died   26 February 1950 (aged 79)
              Strathaven, Lanarkshire, Scotland, UK

Occupation Music hall comedian & singer

10.

"Keep right on to the end of the road"
Sir Harry Lauder
"Sounds like the sound track to my dad's life" – John Leggate

11.

Private John Leggate
Royal Field Artillery
Royal Horse
1914 - 1918 - 1921

12.

13. Young Madge. Studio shot in Tottenham

14. Young Madge with two school-friends

15. Madge and her friend Doris

16. Madge's Grandma Helen Burns (the O'Grady side of the family) with a child who died young, but had she lived, she would have been Madge's aunt Katie

17. Madge's mum Sophie in 1918.
Portland Studio. Tottenham High Road, WW1,
She preferred to be called Sophie,
although her birth certificate recorded her name as Sophia

18. Madge's mum and dad Steve and Sophie
on a walk in the countryside

19. Uncle Mick Burns from the Burns side of Madge's family Madge said the shot was just like she remembered him.

20. My brother John Leggate RN Chief Petty Officer Guns

21. Posthumous Arctic Star medal for service on the Arctic convoys applied for

22. A crew-mate of mine called McChesney
and his friend (name un-remembered).
I happily swapped my 'Far East posting'
for McChesney's posting which was to the UK.
His friend was already being posted to the Far East

23. A shot of me at 19 years old which was taken in the Wolstenholme Studio at 33 Coronation Street, Blackpool They billed themselves as specialists in Out Door Work.

24. That's me, Bulls-Eye Bill, at a funfair shooting gallery in Blackpool
Apparently if you hit the bull a photo was taken automatically

25. Me mid-back row. RAF Gunnery School at Pembrey in Wales prior to being posted to Nassau

26. Accommodation on board the New Amsterdam
USN archive

27. "Bananas in the Bahamas".
Me, Jock Faulkner and Wally Shaw
on the beach in Nassau. 1944/45

28. Me, Jock Faulkner and Wally Shaw in "summer kit". Nassau

29. Full ten-men crew of Liberator. I'm middle row on left
Wally Shaw has a row to himself

30. Diving Platform on Paradise Beach

31. RAF Boxing team. Nassau, Bahamas.
I am in the back row fifth from the left.

32. My friend Wally Charles
of Bomber Command.
Taken early 1945 at his home
in Islington in the
East End of London.
Wally was killed shortly after
on a raid on Germany

33. Me play-acting at Christmas 1944,
round the back of the Mess in Nassau

The photo was probably taken by Jock Faulkner

34. Wallis Simpson – The Duchess of Windsor
at a garden party at Government House in Nassau

35. Our wedding portrait. St. George's Church. Enfield Wash.

36. Mum and Dad far left, bridesmaid Doris, best man Harry Rodda, Madge's mum and dad

37. Very young John taken at Madge's parent's house in Enfield.
From left: Madge, her mum and friend Olive

38. Leggate family with four of our boys.

39. The young Leggate gang plus their 'moll' – girl's name unknown

40. Madge in New York

41. John received the CBE – with Madge, John and Barbara and family

42. Madge's diary

43.

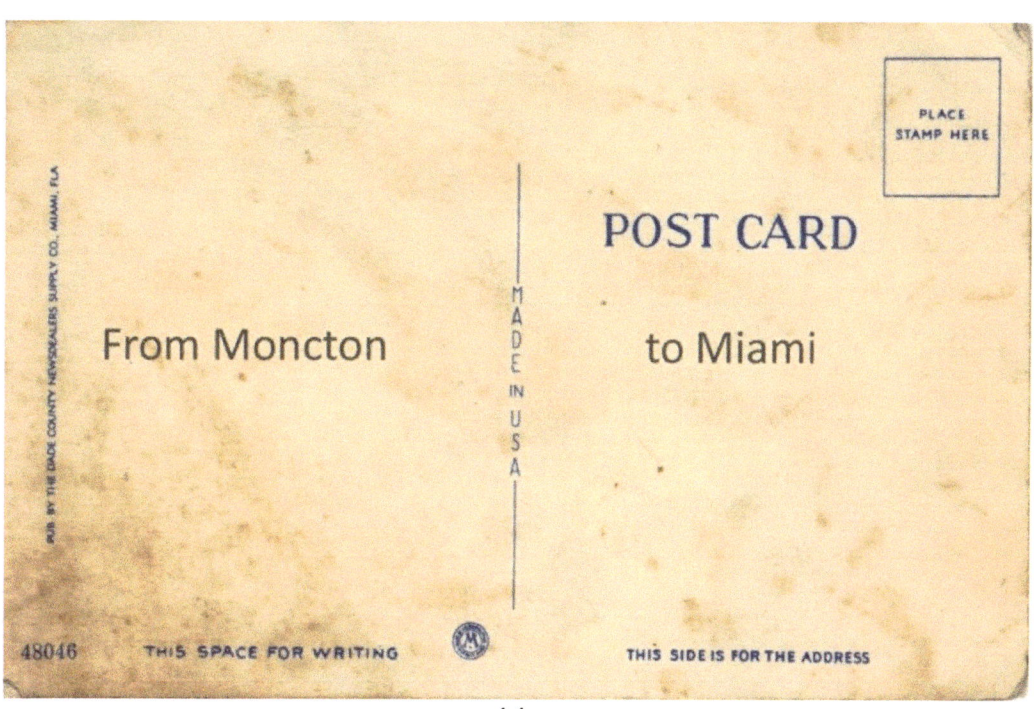

44.

45. Italo Balbo's epic formation flight from Rome to Chicago

46.

1. Strathaven   2. Lough Foyle

From Pony Boy to Paradise Beach 184

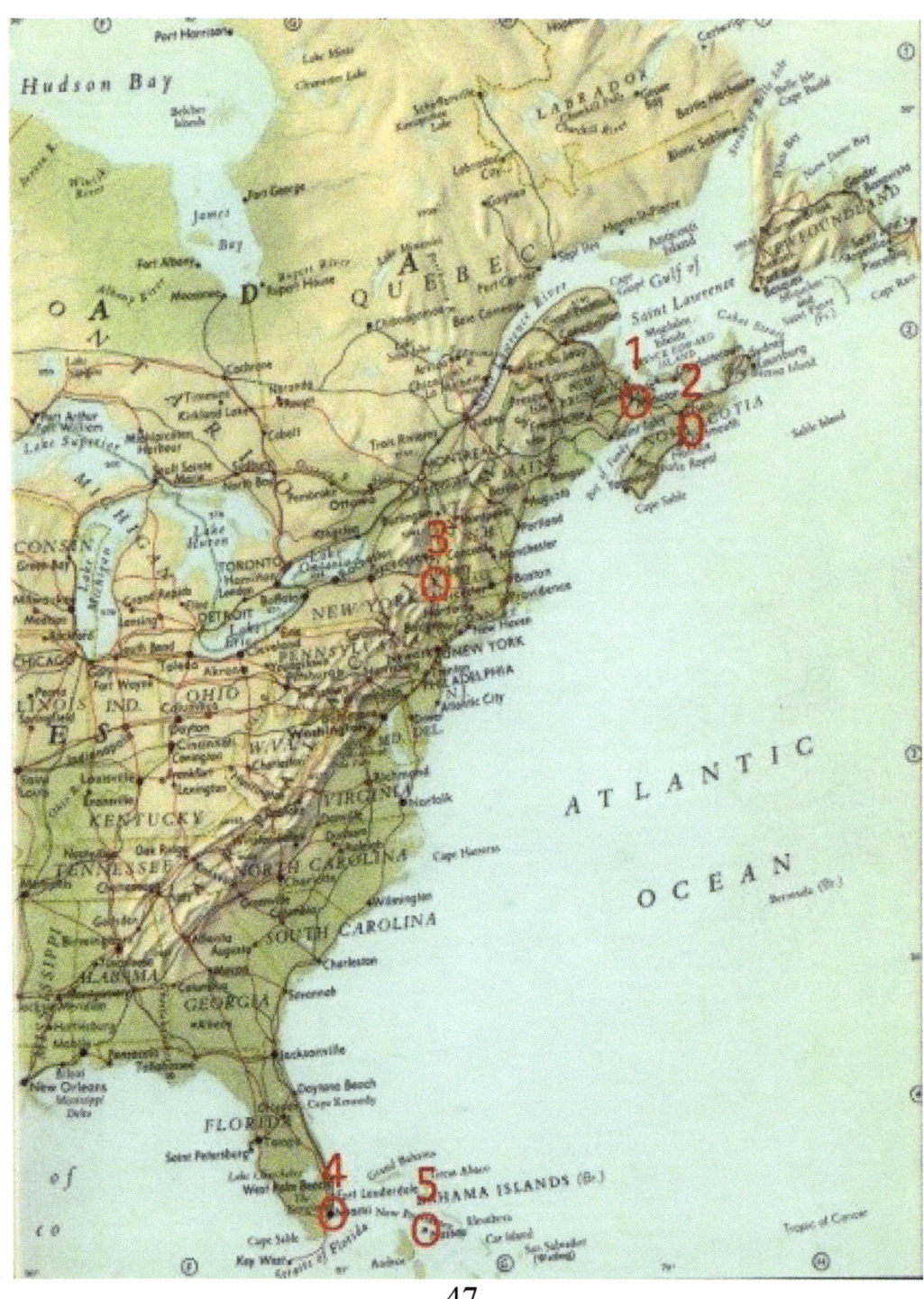

47.

1. Moncton
2. Halifax
3. Albany
4. Miami
5. Nassau